A CENTURY OF
HARLEY - DAVIDSON

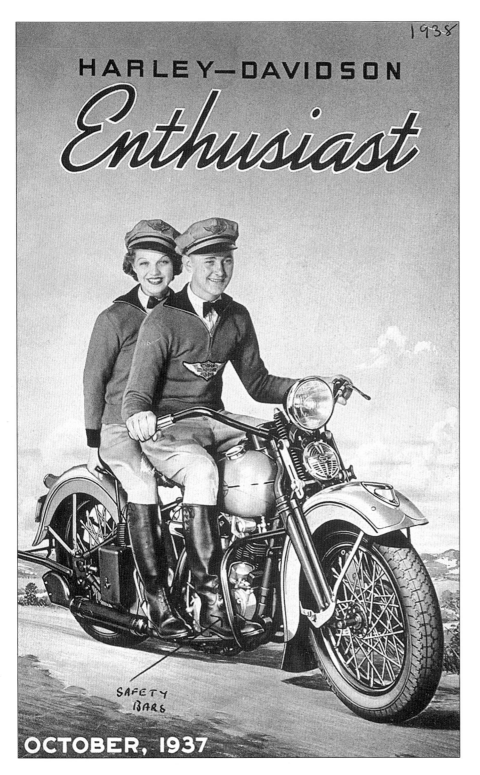

1938

HARLEY—DAVIDSON
Enthusiast

SAFETY BARS

OCTOBER, 1937

A CENTURY OF
HARLEY - DAVIDSON

PETER HENSHAW

Grange
BOOKS

Published in 1998 by
Grange Books
An imprint of Grange Books Plc.
The Grange
Kingsnorth Industrial Estate, Hoo, nr. Rochester, Kent
ME3 9ND

Printed in China

A Century of Harley-Davidson **represents the private
view of the author and is not an official Harley-
Davidson publication.**

All colour photography is supplied by Garry Stuart.
Archive material is reproduced by kind permission of
Harley-Davidson United Kingdom.

Motorcycle, icon, or both? The Harley-Davidson's appeal transcends generations and national boundaries and is revered by people who have never even ridden a motorcycle.

Contents

Introduction

As the Harley-Davidson Motor Company approaches its 100th birthday, its future seems secure. It has the highest of profiles, queues of potential buyers, large profits and plans for expansion. The Harley-Davidson is not just a motorcycle: it is more a mobile icon, sought for the way it looks and sounds and feels and for what it represents, rather than as a means of simply getting from A to B. Advertising agencies love it, glorifying it as the ultimate expression of freedom out on an open road which stretches straight to the horizon under big, blue skies. In the eyes of many, even those who have never ridden any kind of motorcycle – let alone a Harley – it remains the ultimate. In terms of image, Harley-Davidson is the best in the business, highly successful and the Real Thing.

In fact, because that image is so powerful, the Harley's many other attributes, if not fading into insignificance, have at least begun to assume relatively less importance. It can be compared to the Morgan sportscar, which is bumpy, noisy, draughty and not that quick. However, this traditional roadster looks as if it came straight out of the 1930s and Morgan buyers have to wait about five years for the privilege of taking delivery of one. There is an essential difference, however. Morgan makes one or two cars a day, Harley currently outsells the entire European motorcycle industry; but in both cases you are buying the same thing – nostalgia.

But it wasn't always like this. Over the years, Harleys have been derided as outdated, unreliable and full of vibration – heavy, oily anachronisms that have no place in the modern world. Neither have they always been commercial successes. Not only did the four founders (that's three Davidsons and one Harley) consider closing

down in the early thirties, but the company was days away from collapse as recently as 1985.

And these weren't isolated troubles: the cut-throat competition with Indian in the difficult twenties and thirties and the post-war period when first British then Japanese motorcycles knocked Harley off its pedestal, ousted it from its position as a mainstream leader to producer of motorcycles for a niche market, which in a sense it still remains. In the sixties, its association with Aermacchi brought its own headaches when the company ran out of money, was forced to go public and finally agree to a takeover. As for the seventies – the AMF days – Harley sold a lot of bikes without having such a good reputation for quality.

Underlying this, and the cause of a good deal of it, was the fact that Harley-Davidson has always been a conservative company, resistant to change and not given to risk-taking. Right from the start, it was Willam Harley and Arthur Davidson's wish to make a straightforward, reliable motorcycle – no frills, no wild innovations, just solid good value for money – and this philosophy stood them in good stead in the early years of their endeavours.

Chapter One
The 1900s:
In the Beginning

**The first prototype – Assemble a few – Strength through development – Soaring sales –
The first V-twin, the first failure**

*Harley-Davidson had no desire to make the
fastest motorcycle money could buy, nor the
flashiest, nor the most advanced, but it did
have to work, and keep on working ...*

The world in which William Harley and the
Davidson brothers grew up was one of
optimism and belief in the growing technology.
Steam power had already transformed Europe
and the United States, and the advent of
electricity and the internal combustion engine
promised easier lives for many and fortunes for a
few. The destructive power of technology had yet
to be experienced in two world wars, as were the
effects of global pollution. Instead, trade was
increasing and people were travelling more than
ever. After centuries of reliance on actual horsepower the world was now seeing the first
glimpses of the mechanical kind. These were
exciting times for all and it is no coincidence that
in 1903 the Wright brothers tested their first
powered aircraft, the Model A Ford was
launched, and the first Harley-Davidson
motorcycle was sold.

Neither was it a coincidence that all these
three events occurred in North America. Still
young enough to warrant the epithet 'New
World', America still beckoned as the land of
opportunity for many Europeans, among them
the Harleys from Manchester, and the Davidsons
(a Scottish family, from Aberdeen), who had
crossed the Atlantic in the late 19th century and
fortuitously settled very close to each other, in
Milwaukee, Wisconsin. Perhaps if the Davidsons
had simply moved south to Manchester, then the
Harley-Davidson would have been a British bike,
though such speculation, however interesting, is
ultimately pointless.

By 1903, it must have seemed to the
Davidson parents that their sons had already gone
their separate ways. The eldest, William, was
foreman with the Milwaukee Road railroad
company while Walter had moved to Kansas, to
work as a machinist. Meanwhile, young Arthur
remained in Milwaukee and struck up a
friendship with one William Harley. But within a
few years, all four of them would be working on
a project that would unite them for the rest of
their lives.

It was natural that Bill Harley and Arthur
should become friends; both worked at the Barth
Manufacturing Company (Arthur was a
patternmaker, Bill a draughtsman); both were
interested in fishing and cycling, and in the up-
and-coming internal combustion engine. Whether
or not you believe either of the stories that they
decided to develop an engine to help pace cycle
races, or maybe to power their row-boat out to
better fishing grounds, the two began to spend all
their free time doing just that. Crucial to their
early experiments was Emile Kruger, a German,
who also worked at Barth but had practical
experience of the De Dion engine. With his help,
Bill and Arthur built their first engine and, as
many others were doing at the time, bolted it to a
bicycle frame.

Like most similar devices of the time, it was
tiny and crude. It measured about 10 cubic inches
(164cc), and speed was controlled not by the
basic carburettor, but by changing the spark
setting. It was Ole Evinrude (another yet-to-be-
famous name) who helped Bill and Arthur
develop a carburettor that worked. Having
persuaded Walter to abandon Kansas (it was said
that they offered him a ride on the new
motorcycle, but he arrived to find he was

Period travel of the early years is personified in this elegant wickerwork sidecar. Motorcycles were a utilitarian form of transport then, and the simple, reliable Harley-Davidson single acquitted itself well in the role.

expected to assemble it first), their first prototype was completed in the spring of 1903.

For many keen young entrepreneurs, this would have been the cue to rush straight into production – they had a working motorcycle, after all. But Harley and the Davidsons were of sterner stuff. Their first concern was to test the bike to destruction, strengthen it, and test it again. In any case, there is no evidence that this first prototype was intended to be the basis of a business venture – all three kept their full-time jobs – and if a friend had not asked them to build a replica for him later that year, that is probably how it would have remained.

It must have been a busy year. That first prototype lacked power as well as strength, so Bill designed a new, larger engine of 25ci (410cc), still on the same four-stroke De Dion principles, with an atmospheric inlet valve. It had

enough power, but quickly vibrated the flimsy bicycle frame to pieces. The only answer was a purpose-built frame – in other words, a true motorcycle. It carried no great innovations. Like its contemporaries, the first Harley-Davidson had no clutch or gears, but a simple leather belt transmission; there was no suspension either, and to start it, you pedalled, as you would the bicycle it still resembled.

Not innovative, perhaps, but reliable. So reliable, that a Mr. Meyer bought the 25-ci prototype and rode 6,000 miles before selling it to George Lyon who added another 15,000. Then a Dr. Webster bought the machine, then Louis Fluke, then Stephen Sparrow. By 1913, this spindly contraption had travelled over 100,000 miles (161,000km) under its various owners and, according to the company, was still on its original bearings. This incredible feat seemed to

amply confirm the founders' initial philosophy. They had no desire to make the fastest motorcycle money could buy, nor the flashiest, nor the most advanced, but it did have to work, and keep on working.

Interest was generated and orders for the new Harley-Davidson began to appear, but still the pair refused to rush into anything. William Davidson, the Scottish carpenter, built a 10 x 8-ft (3 x 2.5-m) shed in the back garden with 'Harley-Davidson Motor Co.' on the door. With an eye to the future, Bill Harley left Barth's to study for an engineering degree, reasoning that if they were to go into business, they might as well do it properly. Meanwhile, over the winter, Arthur built up two bikes for customers and early the following year, Walter left Kansas for good to make bikes full-time.

The little shed was doubled in size and some part-time help was employed. But they still only made three machines that year, and five the year after. It wasn't until 1906 that a loan from a rich uncle of the Davidsons – James McLay – enabled them to build a small factory on Chestnut Street (later to become Juneau Avenue). One snag emerged almost immediately – railway surveyors objected that the framework of the new shed encroached on their right of way by 18 inches. The solution was simple: ten strapping fellows picked up the frame, shifted it back again, and honour was satisfied. The factory was completed where it stood, turned out 49 bikes that same year, and in somewhat enlarged form still turns out Harley-Davidson engines to this day.

This success encouraged Arthur to quit his day job and devote his energies full-time; he also embarked on a project which set Harley-Davidson apart from its contemporaries, some of whom sold bikes mail-order, while others bought in frames and engines, bolted the assemblages together and crossed their fingers. Harley-Davidson not only had its own bike, but put a lot of effort into recruiting dealers who could service its bikes as well as sell them. Arthur was a born salesman and was soon out on the road doing what he did best. The dealer network was to become one of the company's great strengths – not that relations between the two were always cordial.

Meanwhile, production grew in leaps and bounds: output tripled to 152 machines in 1907, and tripled again the following year. By now there were enough workers on the payroll to justify a factory manager, and the eldest Davidson brother was the obvious choice. The four founders were now in place, and they were to lead Harley-Davidson for the next 40 years. At the same time the company was officially incorporated, and all four gained impressive job titles: Bill Harley (still away at college, though closely in touch) was Chief Engineer, Walter President, and Arthur Sales Manager, while their elder brother became Works Manager. Harley-Davidson Incorporated was born.

It was a period of frantic activity for them all. William kept on adding to the factory to meet rocketing demand, and his son later recalled him installing machinery and starting production as soon as the cement was dry. Bill Harley returned from college, degree in hand, but first went to Chicago with Walter to learn oxyacetelyne welding in order to instruct the growing workforce. Meanwhile, few changes had been made to the bike's original 1903 form. Known as the 'Silent Gray Fellow' (owing to its quiet running and now standard grey colour) it was time for an update. Most significant were the sprung forks: Harley designed a set of strong leading link forks which, unlike rival cartridge forks, did not vary the wheelbase as they worked. Four coil springs did the business, and the whole assembly was strong, rigid and worked well. So well, that the same basic design endured for 40 years, and (in redesigned form) reappeared in the late eighties.

The following year, the whole bike was enlarged into the 5-35, now with a 35ci (574cc) 5hp engine, longer wheelbase and larger frame, though it retained the old belt-drive. If there remained any doubt about Harley-Davidson's reliability, Walter silenced it in 1908 by winning the Long Island Endurance Run with a perfect score, and followed it up with 188mpg (67km per litre) in an economy run the week after. That Long Island event did Harley Davidson no end of good in an age when many motorcycles were an even less reliable form of transport than the early automobiles.

In its latest form, Silent Gray Fellow could top 50mph (80km/h), but as the company's mushrooming rivals showed (there were over 30 motorcycle makers in America by this time), this wasn't necessarily enough. In America, where journeys were long, the little single-cylinder

RIGHT
The 25ci single was the
company's first production
engine.

BELOW
The 1912 single (though not,
strictly speaking, belonging to
this chapter) was little changed
apart from receiving sprung
forks and a longer (35ci) engine.

OPPOSITE, RIGHT
A 1905 Silent Gray Fellow: a
quiet, well-mannered bike (by
contemporary standards).

pioneer motorcycle simply wasn't big enough.
Fortunately, there was a very simple answer – the
V-twin.

Bill Harley, strange as it may now seem, did
not invent the V-twin: when he designed Harley-
Davidson's version he was simply following
current industrial trends. And there were many
very good reasons for choosing the V-twin route.
It involved minimal redesign as it was possible to
double up existing singles onto a beefed-up
crankcase; it fitted neatly into the bicycle-derived
diamond frame; best of all, it promised a near
doubling of power for little more weight and cost.

Unfortunately, Harley-Davidson's first
attempt at a twin didn't quite work out as
planned. There is evidence that a prototype was
built in 1907, but the first production bikes failed

to live up to their promise. Still saddled with atmospheric inlet valves (that is, valves opened by suction rather than mechanically), the twin continued to be limited to about 500rpm which, with the same gearing as the single, meant it was no faster. Even so, the 49ci (803cc) twin's extra power was enough to make the leather drivebelt slip, so you had the worst of both worlds. It was withdrawn from sale for a year or so, while Bill returned to the drawing board.

It was his, and Harley-Davidson's, first real setback, but the fact that such a flawed engine made it to production at all was in odd contrast to the care and patience with which the original single had been developed. This spectre of insufficient development was to haunt Harley-Davidson for decades to come. Still, the single's

meteoric rise was unaffected: sales more than doubled to 1,000 in 1909, and over 3,000 bikes left the factory the following year. In just a few years the company had become a major player in the U.S. motorcycle industry – not bad for what began as a small concern with two men and a homemade shed.

Specifications

1906 Silent Gray Fellow
Engine

Type	Single cylinder, inlet-over-exhaust, atmospheric inlet valve
Bore x stroke	3.125 x 3.50in
Capacity	26.8ci (440cc)
Piston	Solid skirt, three rings
Lubrication	Total loss, metered through needle valve

Transmission

Clutch	None
Gearbox	None
Final drive	1.125in leather belt

Chassis

Suspension	None
Wheelbase	51in (130cm)
Weight	185lb/84kg (est.)
Fuel capacity	1.5 gallons (7 litres)
Oil capacity	4 pints (2.3 litres)
Top speed	45mph (72km/h)

ABOVE
Harley-Davidson's first twin was a disappointment, but better was to come.

LEFT
The first twin's atmospheric inlet valves were what held it back.

OPPOSITE
A highly restored single with non-original paintwork.

Chapter Two
The 1910s:
What Could Go Wrong?

**The V-twin is developed – The brief age of innovation – Wrecking Crew racers make their mark –
Doing well out of the war – The Sport Twin – Borrowed money**

Indian still led the field by a long chalk, but Harley was catching up fast.

If Harley and the Davidsons had been premature in launching their V-twin, they did not repeat the mistake. When the twin reappeared as the F-type in 1911, it was ready to go, and was to stay in production with few fundamental changes for 17 years. This time, Bill Harley completed the job: the new twin had pushrod-operated inlet valves so that it could rev higher and produce more power, and the drive belt was tensioned to reduce slippage. Actually, only 6.5hp was claimed for the F twin as opposed to 7hp for the abortive 1909 version. The difference was that all the 1911 horses were present and correct.

The first F-type was still 49ci (803cc), but a 61ci (1000cc) option (which soon became standard) was offered the following year. There was a decent Bosch magneto, while Harley-Davidson's own Springer forks carried over, as did the total-loss lubrication. The latter was typical of the day – oil trickling gravitationally down to the crankcase for the crank and bearings. It was then sucked up the cylinder walls into the combustion chamber, and any excess was either drained periodically from the crankcase, or simply burned off. It served its purpose, if you didn't mind a little smoke, and was supplemented in 1912 by a hand-operated oil pump so that you could lend a helping hand when the motor was working hard.

Primitive as these machines now seem, they were actually part of a short-lived golden age of innovation for American motorcycles. From 1910 up to about 1915/16, there were a flurry of innovations that put such bikes ahead of the equivalent Europeans. The reason isn't hard to find: to cope with the conditions at home, American machines had rapidly gained in power and size, so the performance limitation of single-speed belt-drive, for example, was thrown into starker relief than it was in Europe. The golden age was short-lived, however; just as America was first with larger motorcycles, so it was with cheap mass-produced cars that all but killed off the non-enthusiast market.

The up-and-coming Harley-Davidson company was swept along in the tide of these innovations, even if it wasn't always first to come up with them. A basic clutch (Harley-Davidson called it an 'idler') in the rear hub allowed the rider to stop and start without lurching to a halt before having to laboriously pedal to start the engine again. But that was short-lived, as Bill Harley had been working on a proper multi-plate item which allowed the simultaneous option of chain-drive. Part of the package was a two-speed gear in the hub – three sets of bevel gears were controlled by a hand lever on the left of the tank. As long as they were greased every 1,500 miles (2,414km), they worked well, and with variable gears the motor could be tuned for more power as it no longer had to be as flexible as a steam engine. By this time, Harley-Davidson was guaranteeing 11hp from every twin, and one made 16.7hp – more than twice the original.

The same year saw a proper kick starter on the twin so that you didn't have to pedal bicycle-fashion to start the engine. There was another breakthrough in 1915 when a three-speed sliding gear transmission was mounted behind the engine, with a primary chain driving the clutch.

Year by year, all the essentials of the modern motorcycle were coming into being. The drip-feed lubrication had also had its day, and the

1915 twins boasted a fully automatic oil pump which would keep the engine supplied with lube without any interference from the rider, albeit at a modest 4psi. This was no bad thing, as the tendency with a hand pump was for over-anxious owners to overdo it, forcing excess oil into the combustion chamber. The hand pump was still there for 'emergencies' or for conservative owners who refused to trust the new-fangled, out-of-sight auto pump – though now with a locking device. The latter was apparently useful when parked in town as inquisitive small boys had been know to play with the hand pump while the owner's back was turned, filling the crankcase with oil.

The final innovation of an eventful 1915 was electric lighting. Twins so equipped were J models, and used a gear-driven magneto-generator. It wasn't just a basic system either, as the rear light could be removed and used as an inspection light, while a vacuum-operated switch allowed current to the lights only while the engine was running, making it impossible to

walk off and leave them on.

By this time the V-twin had surpassed the single as Harley-Davidson's main product. The single had not been neglected – it too acquired chain-drive and the three-speed transmission – but it was clear which way the market was going. And only ten years after Bill and Arthur's first prototype wobbled onto the streets of Milwaukee, their young company was rapidly becoming one of the major players. They sold just over 3,000 motorcycles in 1910, well over 5,000 the year after and over 9,000 the year after that. Over 16,000 were sold as war broke out in Europe and 22,000 as the decade came to a close.

But good though the figures looked, they were part of a motorcycle market that was beginning to level off. Henry Ford's T wasn't yet at its rock bottom price, but it could be bought on instalments, dealing a mortal blow to the motorcycle and sidecar as family transport, at least in America. In 1913, there were 35 makes of American motorcycle, but many began to fall by the wayside, unable to compete on quality, dealer

Although Harley-Davidson built and sold countless passenger sidecars, many others went to the U.S. Mail or, in this case, to the Russian front.

spread or price. Those who survived had a much larger slice of the same cake and of these, three companies dominated. The giant Indian still led the field by a long chalk, but Harley was catching up fast, and both were leaving Excelsior well behind. The almost legendary rivalry between Milwaukee and Springfield had begun, and was to last for 30 years.

Perhaps it was the desire to challenge Indian that persuaded the founders to finally sanction racing although they had always had an ambivalent attitude towards it – Walter's 1908 victory being a special case in that it was an endurance event. In the first place, it had never been their aim to make the world's fastest motorcycle, and an advertising campaign of 1911 set out more typical Harley-Davidson priorities. 'The Harley-Davidson', it stated, 'is the most desirable motorcycle for general use ... it is the most Comfortable ... the most Economical ... the most Reliable ... the most Durable ... the Easiest-Starting.' The Harley-Davidson had a reputation, not as the outlaw's rip-roaring sportster (that was to come) but as a solid and sensible means of transport.

This didn't stop certain Harley enthusiasts racing on their own account, and sometimes winning, and by 1913 (the same year that one advertisement stated, 'we do not believe in racing ... ') the founders bit the bullet and made it official. William Ottaway, the clever engineer from Thor, was taken on to develop factory racers. His II-K was based on the J twin, but used different cams and porting with a shorter wheelbase frame. It was capable of over 90mph (145km/h), which was too much for the Springer fork, but the founders wouldn't allow Ottaway to design something more suitable.

But after the first race victories, in 1915, they did allow him to keep working on engines, and the following year Ottaway came up with the Model 17 8-valve racer. It was developed with the aid of British engineer Harry Ricardo, but only after a struggle – cautious Walter apparently objected to the cost of his steamboat ticket. Ricardo was worth the price, as the 8-valve bike was soon turning out 55hp. The racers (and a single-cylinder version) went into limited production and, as they won races, sold to eager customers. Meanwhile, the factory team – the 'Wrecking Crew' – was notching up firsts at board tracks all over America, while Harleys

were racing at Brooklands as well. But the whole effort was disbanded in 1921, when falling sales caused corporate horns to be hurriedly drawn in.

But we are getting ahead of ourselves. The racing was all very well but, as war broke out in Europe, Harley-Davidson was still some way behind Indian in both sales and dealer spread. The war was to change all that, and it happened like this. At first, for the U.S. manufacturers, the conflict in Europe simply meant a drying up of certain useful components, such as Bosch electrics. What really changed everything was the United States' entry into the war in 1916. This being the first major mechanized war the world had seen, the manufacturers were called upon to supply solos and (mainly) sidecar outfits. The sidecars were used for despatch and reconaissance, or as mobile machine-guns.

Indian threw itself into the war effort with a patriotic fervour, turning over its entire production to the needs of the military, and supplying 41,000 bikes up to 1918. Harley and the Davidsons, on the other hand, displayed their usual caution. They made sure to keep back enough bikes to service the home market and keep their dealers happy. Meanwhile, some disgruntled Indian dealers were left with nothing to sell, and Arthur lost no time in recruiting them. He was also consolidating the company's

control over its own dealers, weeding out the less effective ones and instigating a network of factory representatives across the country, which allowed tighter control from the centre. As the years went by, the dealers began to see a Harley-Davidson franchise as a mixed blessing. When a new model had teething troubles (and they did), dealers were often expected to put things right. And the factory continued to keep a tight rein on what dealers could and could not sell. It was (at least in those days) more of a love-hate relationship than one big happy family.

But in spite of the difficulties encountered by Harley-Davidson dealers, it must have all seemed worthwhile as peace returned to Europe and American soldiers began to return home. In 1914, Milwaukee made just over 16,000 bikes – in 1919 it was well over 22,000 (not to mention 16,000-odd sidecars). There was no doubt about it: Harley-Davidson was the success story of the motorcycle industry.

In fact, it was doing so well with the V-twins that everyone was most surprised when Harley-Davidson announced something completely different in 1919 – the Sport Twin. Well, it was certainly a twin, but the 'Sport' part was open to debate. Unlike the large heavyweight V-twins which had made Harley-Davidson's name and which dominated the U.S. market, the 'W' was a

quiet, mild-mannered horizontally-opposed twin
of 37ci (600cc). It was small (53.5-inch/136-cm
wheelbase), lightweight (275lb/125kg) and easy
to ride. It certainly wasn't outdated either, with
an enclosed chain, three-speed gearbox and
option of electric lighting. In fact, it was just
what certain commentators had said was needed
– basic transport for the man in the street who
couldn't even afford one of Mr. Ford's four-
wheelers.

But it was not to be. There was now a decent
supply of secondhand Model Ts for those who
couldn't afford a new one, and the Sport Twin
failed to attract a new untapped audience to
motorcycling. As for the established U.S. riders,
the bike was simply too slow, with a top speed of
50mph (80km/h) and 40mph (64km/h) when
cruising. That it was quiet and smooth mattered
not – real motorcycles were V-twins and let you
know it in no uncertain terms. It was different in
Europe though, and the Sport Twin was well
received in England, Belgium, Holland and
Scandanavia. The English success was

particularly apposite as the Sport Twin was
unashamedly inspired by the Bristol-built
Douglas, another fore-aft horizontal twin of
about the same size.

In fact, this is an interesting point which
highlights Harley-Davidson's fundamental
conservatism. It was V-twins (and to a lesser
extent singles) that had made the company what it
was and it sought only to make simple,
uncomplicated bikes that formed the backbone of
the U.S. market. Whenever it felt the need to stray
from this familiar territory, it looked elsewhere
for inspiration rather than beginning again with a
clean sheet of paper. When it did come close to
making a four (a V4 designed by Everett DeLong
in the mid-twenties) it was based heavily on J
twin components but, in any case, William
Davidson vetoed it as too costly to make.

Thus the Sport Twin owed much to the
Douglas. The 21ci (344cc) single (1926) came in
direct response to Indian's very similar Prince
which in turn was based on British singles of the
time. We can probably make allowances for the

World War II BMW-based flat twin XA – the military wanted a shaft-drive flat twin just like the Germans' – so that's what they got. Post-war, the little two-stroke Hummer was really a pre-war DKW (BSA did the same thing and called it the Bantam). And the Aermacchi bikes of the sixties and early seventies wore Harley badges but were in fact made in Italy.

None of these alternatives remotely approached the success of Milwaukee's V-twins, serving to reinforce the company's devotion to this familiar pattern. Certainly, for the last 20 years, the company has made nothing but V-twins, and it is now so closely identified with them as to make anything else seem a sacrilege.

But though the Sport Twin was ridiculed at home as a baby bike, it was certainly tough. The year it was announced, Harley's new publicity manager, Julian ('Hap') Scherer, rode one from the Canadian border to New Mexico, covering the 1,700-odd miles (2,736km) in just under 65 hours, and breaking the record. He broke the Denver to Chicago record the following spring

Specifications

Sport Twin
Engine

Type	Horizontally-opposed twin, side-valve
Bore x stroke	2.75 x 3.00in (70 x 76mm)
Capacity	35ci (574cc)
Compression ratio	3.75:1 (est.)
Power	6bhp

Transmission

Clutch	Wet, multiplate
Gearbox	Three-speed, sliding gears
Final drive	Enclosed chain

Chassis

Suspension	Front: trailing link Rear: none
Wheelbase	57in (145cm)
Weight	250lb (113kg)
Seat height	9.5in (75cm)
Fuel consumption	70mpg/25km per litre (claimed)
Top speed	50mph/80km/h (est.)

Specifications

1915 J twin
Engine

Type	45-degree V-twin, ioe
Bore x stroke	3.625 x 3.50in (92 x 89mm)
Capacity	60.3ci (988cc)
Lubrication	Total loss, with automatic oil pump and supplementary hand pump

Transmission

Clutch	Dry, multiplate
Gearbox	Three-speed, sliding gears
Final drive	Chain

Chassis

Suspension	Front: leading link Springer fork Rear: none
Wheelbase	59.5in (151cm)
Weight	325lb (147kg)
Fuel capacity	1.9 gallons (8.6 litres)
Oil capacity	5 pints (2.8 litres)
Fuel consumption	50mpg/18km per litre (est.)
Top speed	60mph/97km/h (est.)

OPPOSITE, ABOVE
The Sport Twin was an unsuccessful attempt to open up a new market for a popular motorcycle for non-enthusiasts.

BELOW
Brass hats and other ranks inspect machine-gun-equipped Harley outfits c. 1917. But the realities of trench warfare made such mobility less vital.

and a naturalist called Edwin Hogg rode one through Death Valley, with no more serious occurrences than a lot of punctures. Still, next to an Indian Scout, the W seemed out of step with the rest of the market and, despite the export success, was dropped after three years.

The Sport Twin was Harley-Davidson's first domestic flop. Since 1903, sales had spiralled ever upwards, year on year. It had caught and virtually surpassed its arch-rival Indian and demand for motorcycles – despite the spectre of cheap cars – was still healthy. So in 1919/20, the founders appeared to forget their natural caution and borrowed heavily ($3 million – a colossal sum at the time) to expand the Milwaukee works. When finished – with over 500,000sq ft (46,450sq m) of space – it was the largest motorcycle factory in the world, and by 1920 was working at almost full capacity, 28,129 Harley-Davidsons being built that year. What could go wrong?

RIGHT
This 1917 outfit was earning its keep in Bengal. Half of Harley-Davidson's production was exported.

BELOW
Passenger sidecars had come on since the old days of wickerwork – this one has both screen and hood – but cheap cars were taking over the role of family transportation.

Chapter Three
The 1920s:
The End of the Honeymoon

Slump and recovery – The Superpowered Twin – A tight rein on dealers – Exports – The V4 Harley – The 21ci singles – The fast Two-Cam – The slow 45 – The troubled VL

Not for the first time had Harley-Davidson launched a bike that was not ready to go on sale. Neither was it to be the last.

If the year 1920 was a high spot for Harley-Davidson, the slump which followed it introduced a new low. There had been teething troubles with the first twin, and the Sport Twin was not well received, but this was the first major hiccup in the path of the company's upward progression from small shed to largest motorcycle factory in the world – all in the space of 10 years. Sales had rocketed every year and Harley-Davidson had clearly waged a canny war, maintaining a foot in the domestic market which Indian had virtually abandoned.

So when sales more than halved in 1921 (only 10,202 that year) it came as a nasty shock to Bill Harley and the Davidsons, especially as they had borrowed $3 million to build their state-of-the-art factory. Not surprisingly, they made their first loss. Displaying a keen sense of business survival, the founders shut the factory for a month and cut all salaries by 15 per cent. They also abandoned the official racing programme. The latter announcement was rather abrupt, being made as the Wrecking Crew was still at the State Fair races at Phoenix, Arizona. According to Harry Sucher in *Harley-Davidson: The Milwaukee Marvel*, the mechanics and machines were shipped back to Milwaukee, but the riders were left stranded and virtually penniless to their own devices! They had to pawn their wristwatches and borrow money from a local Harley-Davidson dealer to raise their train fares home – not a particularly generous treatment of men who had risked their lives transforming the company's image.

They may have been abrupt, but the founders' drastic measures worked. The inventory of unsold bikes melted away and the crisis passed. Jerry Hatfield, in *Inside Harley-Davidson*, maintains that they were even able to repay the big loan that same year. But, although sales did recover, the company followed a fluctuating and uncertain course throughout the twenties and, incredibly, it took over 20 years to match that 1920 sales peak. But these continuing peaks and troughs were not down to general economics. The United States was generally booming throughout the 1920s, once the brief post-war slump was past: but for motorcycles, times were hard.

The reason of course, was the car. There were by now around 400 makes of car available, though what was perhaps more significant was that you could buy a Ford or Chevy for around $400. So the tendency for motorcycles to be regarded less as basic transport than enthusiast's toy, accelerated. Harley-Davidson had already dropped the F-head single, and an indication of the way things were going was the 74ci (1200cc) twin, announced in 1922. Named the Superpowered Twin, it was originally intended as a more efficient sidecar tug, but solo riders welcomed its 18hp. This was a growing niche market for sporting riders for whom a rorty V-twin was the ultimate possession; the Henderson Four might be as powerful, but it was also heavier and didn't have the same inspiring exhaust note. Other than that, little was changed from the original 61ci (1000cc) twin (now 13 years old). The 74 used the same three-speed sliding gear transmission and total-loss oil system, and offered the same choice of magneto (FD) or electric light (JD) equipment.

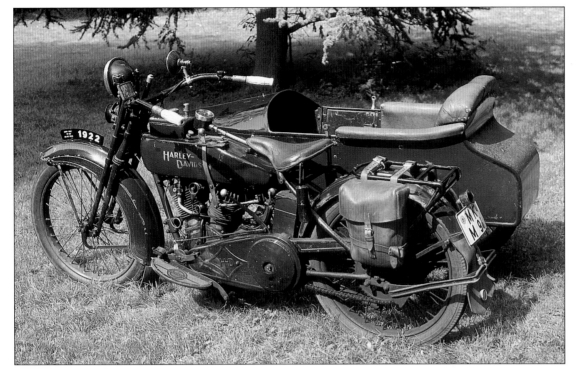

An unrestored original 1922 J-type twin. This was really the bike that consolidated Harley's earlier success, enabling it to catch Indian.

Another means of coping with the tighter competition was to increase control of the dealers. Early on, Harley-Davidson had established an almost ruthless relationship with its dealers (the factory's area representatives were there as much to check that dealers were up to scratch as to help them sell bikes) and now Arthur Davidson took steps to ensure that operations were made completely watertight. Franchise agreements lasted only a year, so every dealer had the ever-present threat of cancellation hanging over their heads. This was fairly common with under-performing dealers, as in the far from healthy motorcycle market there were always plenty of eager candidates ready to assume Harley franchises. An example of this was the situation in Los Angeles, where the Appeal Manufacturing and Jobbing Company had held the Harley-Davidson franchise since 1918. After a few years it was obvious that this particular dealer was not up to scratch, being outsold by both Indian and Excelsior. Some of this was the dealer's own fault (it had no planned sales campaign, and did not advertise) and some was not, as they were located in the vicinity of other rather disreputable dealers. Wherever the fault lay, Arthur Davidson lost little time in offering the Los Angeles franchise to Rich Budelier, who had already made a success of San Diego. The previous dealer was unceremoniously dumped.

There is a footnote to this story: Budelier

offered the job of sales manager to Hap Scherer who, until recently, had been Harley-Davidson's own sales chief. He had been sacked for co-operating in an industrial survey (which ironically, praised Harley-Davidson for its efficiency). On hearing this, Walter Davidson was about to insist that Budelier drop Scherer, when Arthur pointed out that Scherer's good standing among Harley-Davidson enthusiasts made this unwise. Soon after, a new edict was handed down from Milwaukee in which no dealer would be permitted to sell any make apart from Harley-Davidson, not even the little Cleveland, which sold to a completely different market. This was good for Harley-Davidson and Indian (who reluctantly agreed to the deal) but not good for

A 1920 racer. As the years went by, American board track and dirt racers were to move ever further away from their European tarmac-based counterparts.

The F-head Harleys gave a surprisingly good account of themselves in racing, despite the fact that the engine's basic layout dated back to the pioneer days. This is a 1922 61ci (1000cc) version.

the numerous small makes, nor for motorcycling as a whole. It sometimes went further than that. In Denver, Walter Whiting bought Floyd Clymer's Harley-Davidson dealership, building it up into a successful business. The trouble was, he was a good friend of the local Indian dealer, Leslie Richards. The two co-operated in promoting motorcycling, and both sold lots of machines as a result. But to Walter Davidson, this constituted fraternization with the enemy, and when Clymer proposed buying his old franchise back, Whiting was dropped.

So it was tough being a Harley dealer though, if you toed the line, there were rewards to be had, if only because smaller makes were rapidly dropping by the wayside, and Harley-Davidson was becoming the industry's dominant force. Exports played a large role as well. As now, Harleys were sold all over the world – special catalogues for South America had been printed as early as 1913 – and by 1921 there were dealers in 67 countries, while exports absorbed about half of Milwaukee's production. The long association between Harley-Davidson and England began in 1919, when Duncan Watson took over as importer. This was abandoned four years later when new import

tariffs made the American bikes too expensive, but the Harleys had made their mark (not least at Brooklands) and, when unavailable, home-grown equivalents like the JAP and Anzani twins kept European riders happy. A tariff war from 1929 onwards made export ever more difficult, forcing Harley-Davidson back onto its home market.

And the home market was at an interesting point in its history. With Excelsior weakening year by year, Harley and Indian remained the two players of any consequence. But despite their arch-rivalry it made sense for them to co-operate on prices and other matters and thus avoid any damaging competition. Not that it did the buying public, or the smaller manufacturers, much good at all. At the first of these meetings, at a New York hotel in 1922 when, according to Harry Sucher, they were 'savouring crêpes Suzette and lobster thermidor in an atmosphere of strained conviviality', it was agreed to equalize prices and Indian raised its own by $5, to avoid undercutting. It became an annual ritual of a sort, with Frank Weschler and Arthur Davidson meeting to agree prices for the following year. The meetings continued right though the period of Harley-Davidson and Indian's most bitter rivalry, when dealers and police business were

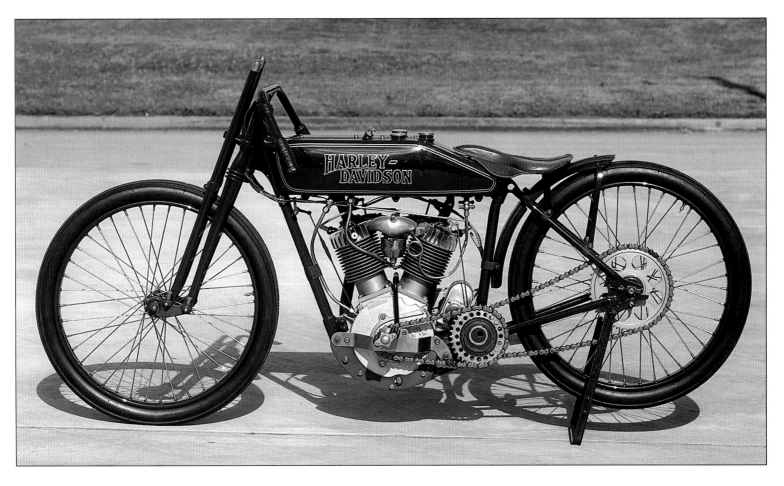

being desperately poached one from another. There was no love lost on either side but the price-fixing agreements were in the interests of them both.

One of Harley's great strengths vis-a-vis Indian was its very simple model range; in the early twenties it was making 61 and 74ci (1000 and 1200cc) V-twins, nothing else. But in 1924 it came close to producing a V4. At the time, most police departments favoured the four-cylinder Henderson which was smoother than the big twins and easier to ride. Harley-Davidson was missing out on the act and drafted in ex-Ace Four designer Everett DeLong. After an initial design was rejected as too expensive by Bill Davidson, DeLong came up with the idea of splicing two J-type twins together. With sleeved-down cylinders it promised a smooth and cool-running V4 of 80ci (1311cc). But despite its use of many current production parts, Bill Davidson again vetoed it on grounds of cost. Since Bill was responsible for Milwaukee's undoubted efficiency, his word carried a lot of weight: the V4 was abandoned and the police got to buy V-twins instead. According to some, the factory was still experimenting with V4s in 1928, one of which reaching the prototype stage, but this

too came to nothing.

One diversion from the V-twin did reach production though. In 1925 Indian launched its 21ci (344cc) single, the Prince (in response to Cleveland dropping its own lightweight). This would never have done, and in short order a Prince, 350cc BSA and a New Imperial were shipped into Milwaukee for evaluation. Shortly afterwards, Harley's own 21ci single appeared, in both side-valve and ohv form. The former was 'A', the latter 'AA'. (It is interesting that, at this stage in its history, the company did not indulge in the frivolity of naming its bikes, unlike Indian. Thus it was Prince vs 'A'; Chief vs 'JD'; Scout vs 'DL'.)

Despite the name (actually, the ohv version was nicknamed the Peashooter), the little single did well: the side-valve job may only have been capable of about 50mph (80km/h), but the price was right and it sold as a straightforward utility bike. It was also far more comfortable than the Prince, retaining Harley-Davidson's sprung seat post. The Peashooter was far livelier – 60mph/97km/h cruising and 65/105 all-out – and did so well in competition that the factory was soon offering a lightened race version, with shorter wheelbase and modified forks. With very

There were 74 cubic inches for the so-called 'Superpowered Twin'. Although intended as a more effective sidecar machine, enthusiastic solo riders welcomed the extra oomph.

few Indian Princes on the scene (the Wigwam was in financial trouble by now) it swept the board in 21ci racing. It was almost like the old Wrecking Crew days, and the Peashooter remained in production for ten years.

Maybe it was this renewed racing success that encouraged Harley-Davidson to come up with the Two-Cam. Also, the side-valve Indians were comprehensively quicker than the ioe Harley-Davidsons, even if they did not hold together so well. However, the Two-Cam certainly did what was required. It used separate cams for each valve thus allowing tuning for more lift, higher compression, higher revs and more power. Available in both 61 and 74 forms, it was described as 'The Fastest Model Ever Offered by Harley-Davidson', which was true enough. They were not cheap ($50 more than the equivalent J) but it was said that a good 74 would top 100mph (161km/h). In the same year, Milwaukee introduced a standard front brake, which was really just as well.

High top speeds were not something one associates with the DL, better known as Harley-Davidson's 45. President Walter Davidson had promised this one to stockholders in late 1927, and production began the following summer. Given that overhead valves were relatively

common by now (particularly in English bikes), designing two new side-valve engines might have seemed a retrograde step. But in the late twenties, ohvs were still oily, messy things which rattled and clacked. They may have been more revvy and powerful, but they wore out more quickly than a side-valve, and Harley-Davidson's reputation was built on cast-iron reliability. Three 45s were offered, a low-compression D, standard DL and high-compression DLD. None of them was fast, and the standard bike could only struggle up to 56mph (90km/h): not only was it far slower than the 75mph (121km/h) Indian Scout (and slower still than the very quick Excelsior Super X), but even Harley-Davidson's own 21ci single could easily outpace it!

A carburettor kit was rushed out to try to improve matters, but even then the 45 proved woefully slow. The Yellowstone Park ordered a fleet of 45s with sidecars attached, only to find that uphills almost defeated them. The sidecars were removed. Nor was this the end of the 45's teething troubles. Someone in the design department had forgotten to leave space for the generator, so it had to be mounted vertically and the bevel gear drive was not unknown to fail. It soon became clear to disgruntled dealers and disappointed riders that this was one Harley that

The JD-type had acquired quite a following, being a well developed bike. Sadly, the new 45ci twin took a while to settle in.

ABOVE
1927, and the J nears the end of its life. The 'Two-Cam' was not a cheap option, but fast.

LEFT
When the side-valve replacement proved disappointing, the faithful urged Harley-Davidson to bring back the J-type. It never did.

had not been extensively road tested. Insult was added to injury when three younger Davidsons (Gordon, Walter and Allan) rode three improved 45s from Milwaukee to Los Angeles. It was intended as a publicity stunt, but the frequent breakdowns made pursuit of this idea inadvisable. In time, of course, the 45 proved to be a solid, reliable performer, powering the G.I.'s favourite WLA and the three-wheeled Servi-Car.

But in 1929, it must have seemed more of an embarrassment. More seriously, and not for the first time, Harley-Davidson had launched a bike that was patently not ready to go on sale. Neither was it to be the last.

It is always difficult to follow a success story, and the J-type twin was certainly that – long-lived and reliable (even fast, in its last Two-Cam form), it was familiar to a whole generation

of riders, and had been the backbone of Harley-Davidson production for nearly 20 years. The side-valve VL that replaced it was almost all new (though bore, stroke and capacity were unchanged) but like the 45 it seemed to have missed out on the development stage altogether. The VL 74 (there was no 61ci/1000cc version) claimed 15–20 per cent more power than the old bike, but the reality was just one horsepower. To

make matters worse, the VL was a real heavyweight – at 529lb (240kg) it weighed 120lb (54kg) more than the J. So Harley-Davidson should not have been surprised when it was slower as well.

In a bid to overcome this (and to keep up with the four-cylinder rivals) the VL had been given small flywheels, which allowed fairly rapid acceleration up to 50mph (80km/h), whereupon it

the midnight oil, came up with the solution. Bigger, heavier flywheels brought out the torque of the engine, as did modified cams. But the bigger flywheels needed bigger crankcases, which in turn needed a bigger frame to accommodate them. In short, all the bikes needed complete rebuilding.

In the end, 1,300 VLs had to have this kit of parts; Harley-Davidson paid for the bits (and it cost them around $100,000) but dealers were expected to rebuild each bike at their own expense. It was another twist in the love-hate relationship between Milwaukee and the dealers. The VLs weren't all bad news – there were nice touches such as interchangeable wheels, decent, reliable electrics and the primary chain was a tough duplex. But there was no getting away from the fact that Harley-Davidson had produced two seriously underdeveloped bikes within two years. Milwaukee's reputation as the maker of solid, reliable motorcycles was severely compromised.

A 1925/26 JD in non-standard livery with a front brake which is also non-standard. It wasn't until well into the thirties that Harley began to offer a range of colours; this was virtually by default and like so much else was inspired by Indian whose Wigwam 21ci single and 45ci Scout made it imperative for Harley-Davidson to rival them. Not until the ohv Knucklehead did Milwaukee make the first move in the game.

Specifications

VL
Engine

Type	45-degree V-twin, side-valve
Bore x stroke	3.42 x 4.00in (87 x 102mm)
Capacity	74ci (1207cc)
Compression ratio	4.5:1 (V, 4:1)
Lubrication	Total loss
Power	30hp @ 4,000rpm (V, 27hp)

Transmission

Clutch	Dry, metal-lined discs
Gearbox	Three-speed, sliding gear
Final drive	Chain

Chassis

Suspension	Front: leading link forks
	Rear: none
Wheelbase	60in (152cm)
Weight	529lb (240kg)
Seat height	28in (71cm)
Fuel consumption	35–50mpg (12–18km per litre)
Top speed	85mph/137km/h (est.)

tailed off alarmingly. They also allowed tooth-loosening vibration at higher speeds and poor hill-climbing/sidecar-pulling ability. So bad were those first bikes that some customers were simply demanding their money back, while others begged that the well-loved J (and the Two-Cam in particular) be brought back. It was time for another fire-fighting redesign, and the engineering department, after much burning of

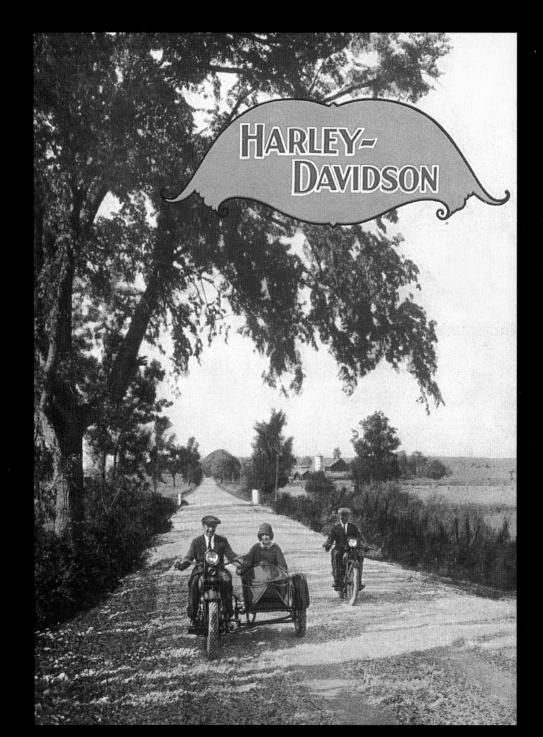

Chapter Four
The 1930s:
A Great Leap Forward

**Slump and recovery (again) – Indian wars – Transformed by the Knucklehead – The Rich Child story –
Petrali and the speed records – The Servi-Car – William dies**

*The Knucklehead didn't just belatedly catch
the opposition – it leapt ahead.*

Every motorcycle manufacturer has a bike
which it recognizes as a milestone in its
history; something so different to that which has
gone before as to completely transform the
company's entire outlook and image. For Harley-
Davidson, there are several contenders for the
title – the first twin, the Sportster, or the
Evolution motor of the early eighties, which
helped Milwaukee in its turnaround from
desperate losses to big profits. But if you are
forced to choose, it must surely be the
Knucklehead. Like all the previous twins, it was
a 45-degree Vee, but there the resemblance ends.
It was otherwise all-new, from the ohv engine to
the four-speed gearbox to the welded-up fuel
tank. Even the traditional Springer fork used
tubular struts rather than I-beams. Most of all, it
transformed Harley-Davidson's image from solid
plodder to performance athlete. The Knucklehead
was a milestone bike all right, but for anyone
attending certain Board meetings in the early
thirties, the biggest surprise would have been that
Harley-Davidson was still around to build it.

In those few years after the 1929 stock-
market crash, Harley-Davidson came closer to
closing than ever before, and the four founders
actually discussed whether they were justified in
persevering with their life-long endeavour. After
all, the various Harley and Davidson families
were financially secure, and the twenties had
been hard for the U.S. motorcycle industry – a
slump followed by ten years of tough
competition, then another slump. They had built
and sold nearly 21,000 bikes in 1929, over
17,000 in 1930, but just 3,703 (one source says

5,689 – whatever, it was a disastrous figure) in
1933. Whether it was loyalty to the workforce
(some of whom had been there since the
beginning) or just the thought of nearly 30 years'
work ending in failure, the founders decided to
carry on. Not only that, they sanctioned the
spending of money and manpower on, what was
for Harley-Davidson, the ground-breaking
Knucklehead.

Men were laid off, salaries were cut by 10
per cent, and the founders cut their own
remuneration by half. Incredibly, they made a
profit in that disastrous year, 1933. They also
proceeded to improve the current range which
had done much to tarnish the Harley-Davidson
image for reliability. The VL gradually gained
both performance and reliability, and once the
early problems were overcome, began to settle
into the role of solid side-valver. A J-type may
have been quicker (especially the Two-Cam) but
a long, fast run would see it overheat or fall by
the wayside – the VL kept going.

The 45 improved too, getting a redesigned
frame in 1932 which allowed the generator to
adopt a conventional position which improved its
reliability no end. To mark the occasion, it was
renamed the 'R' series. Of course, the 45 was
still a slow old thing and, even in 'sporting' DLD
form, was completely outclassed by the Indian
Scout. Still, Indian had suffered recent takeover,
and part of the reorganization involved dropping
the Scout to rationalize production in 1932. It
was to return, but in the meantime the 45 had the
American middleweight market to itself. And the
talent of tuner Tom Sifton even coaxed the 45
into winning a few races: close attention to
porting and valve timing once allowed Sam
Arena to win the Oakland 200. At first Harley-

Davidson was reluctant to give Sifton his due credit. Then it realized what the 45 was capable of and set about developing its own racing version, the WR. Attempts were made to weedle out Sifton's secrets but he refused to be drawn, until 1947, when Sam Arena retired from racing.

Amid those bleak years of the early thirties there had been rumours that Indian was to close. With Excelsior already in a very weak position, this would have left Harley-Davidson with the U.S. motorcycle market all to itself. However, the Wigwam was taken over by millionaire industrialist Paul DuPont, which not only saved Indian but instigated a fresh round of the long-running war between the two companies. Quite apart from some sharp business practice (such as securing prestigious police business by selling machines at virtually cost price) there was an unpleasant side to the whole affair. Some at Milwaukee apparently referred to DuPont as 'that New Jersey Jew' and there was also resentment of DuPont's inherited wealth, the four founders being self-made men. Despite all this, the price-

fixing meetings went on – it was in the interests of both sides to continue them. DuPont apparently turned up at one of these and challenged Harley-Davidson as to its business practices and the prejudices of some of its employees. Arthur Davidson reportedly defended the former and offered a personal apology for the latter. But the damage had been done. It got to the point where local clubs would split into two factions; Wigwams on one side, Hogs on the other.

So many of Harley-Davidson's actions at this time were in direct response to Indian. In 1933 it finally abandoned Olive Green (the standard colour for a decade or so) in favour of a new range of bright colours and stylish graphics. The reason? As part of the DuPont empire, Indian now had access to a range of new paints, and was using them. For Harley buyers it had been a case of any colour you want as long as it was Olive Green – the standard shade since 1918 – and this was consigned to the spares store at last! And it was with one eye on Indian's

By 1933, the VL had settled down. The initial engine problems had been overcome and the clamour to bring back the Two-Cam had now died away.

successful Big Chief that Harley came up with its own direct competitor in 1935. It was the 80ci (1311cc) VLH, the biggest Harley-Davidson yet. Moving the crankpin outboard allowed an increase in stroke to 4.25in (108mm). It was the birth of another classic Harley-Davidson capacity – the 61 and 74 were already in place – which produced 10 per cent more power than the 74. It still had total-loss lubrication though, now completely outmoded. But perhaps one could forgive Harley-Davidson's depleted R&D department, for it was busy enough on the all-new bike that would not just catch Indian, but leapfrog over it.

Work began on the Knucklehead (or 61E, to use the factory's less romantic nomenclature – it would be years before it decided to name its bikes) back in 1931. That it took five years to reach production was as much down to a pruning of the engineering department during those hard times as to any great technical advances. But advanced it was, at least compared to any previous road-going Harley-Davidson. Overhead

valves were not in themselves radical (Milwaukee had been making such engines for years) but the new engine also had a proper recirculating oil system. For the first time on a Harley-Davidson twin you had to change the oil! It also meant a constant supply of fresh, cool oil, better able o cope with long, high-speed runs which the rapidly improving road system made possible. The engine had a shorter stroke than its predecessor (though still undersquare at 3.31 x 3.50in/84 x 89mm) making high speeds possible. In short, the new engine would be able to rev higher than any previous Harley twin, and be comfortable doing so.

As time went on, through all the pay-cuts and doubts concerning the future, work continued. What helped keep the company buoyant at the time was its extraordinary agreement with Alfred Rich Child. Child deserves a biography of his own. Born in Chichester, England, the son of a naval officer, he ran away from home at the age of 16 to work his passage across the Atlantic. Penniless in New York, he

A 1934 VL, now in a range of colours. It successfully assumed the old J's mantle, but not that of the Two-Cam and the new sportster of the range was about to appear.

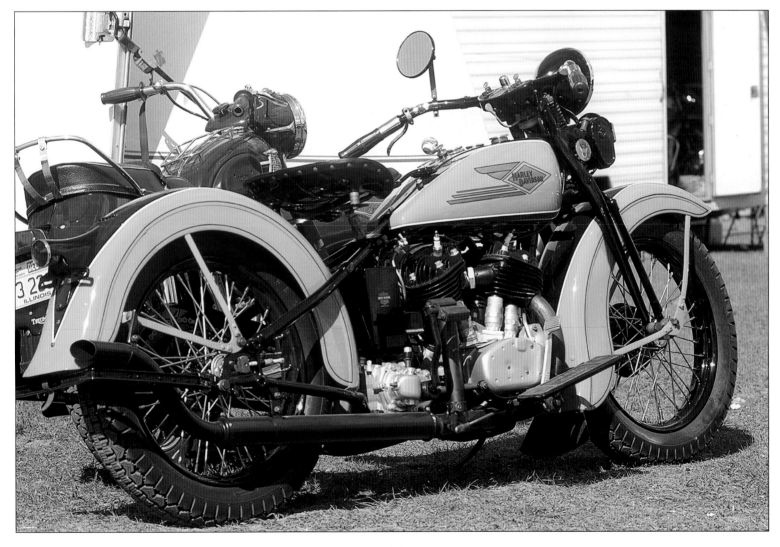

'The Motorcyle with the Fighting Heart' went the slogan, and as far as the 45-degree V-twin was concerned, it was particularly apposite as far as Harley-Davidson was concerned, the layout seeing it through several slumps, powered racers, tourers and sidecar tugs to become the company's trade-mark.

"The Motorcycle with the Fighting Heart"

1. Captain Schmoke of the California Highway Patrol and Rich Budelier, Los Angeles Harley-Davidson dealer, try out a '34, riding "two-up."
2. "The greatest of them all," says Johnny Balmer, Harley-Davidson factory traveler.
3. Shorty Lindstrom of the Knuth Company, Milwaukee, Wis., is mightily pleased with the new 1934—45. "Just right," says Shorty.
4. Arthur Davidson having a chat with M. J. Hinson, Lima, Ohio, dealer, about to leave the factory with his 1934—74 demonstrator.
5. Johnny Loomis, Des Moines, Iowa, dealer, grins happily as he tries out his Big Twin.
6. 101.04 miles per hour! Jim Underwood, Los Angeles, established this new stock machine A. M. A. record with his VLD at Muroc, Cal.
7. I. W. Schroeder, factory representative, samples some 1934 Harley-Davidson horsepower and pronounces it OK. Atta, boy!

soon found work as a maintenance man, and by turns as a butler and travelling salesman. He joined the Coastguard, then the Passport Office where a grateful customer took him onto his own sales force, selling bicycle parts. It was a natural progression to apply to Harley-Davidson for a job. He succeeded, and was sent to sell Harleys in South Africa, where he did a good job, and was despatched to repeat his performance in the Far East. Child managed to set up a healthy import business for Harley-Davidson in Japan which developed into an agreement with a firm called Rikuo, building Harley-Davidsons under licence until well after World War II. The royalties were a source of useful income for Milwaukee at a difficult time and Alfred Rich Child became a rich man.

Back to the Knucklehead. Road testing began in the summer of 1934, when it was immediately apparent that the machine was far from oil-tight. This was partly due to the exposed valve gear (common practice at the time) but also the large number of joints plus the fact that the new oiling system was delivering too much lubrication to certain parts. The planned launch for later that year was abandoned. Testing continued, but the prototypes were now wearing out chains and brake linings too quickly. Some

Board members suggested the whole project be abandoned! Fortunately, wiser counsels prevailed, not least because so much money had already been spent on tooling.

But the problems continued, and as late as 1935, when the founders made the decision to put the bike into production, Joe Petrali (whose racing exploits on Harley-Davidsons were legendary) tried to persuade them to give the engineering department more time. Arthur Davidson was not to be swayed. The 61E had already been delayed a year, and its existence was an open secret. Actually, there was a compromise of sorts: production went ahead in December of that year, but on a limited basis, and dealers were instructed that 'Under no circumstances must this model be ordered as a demonstrator!'

There was no way that dealers and public were going to allow the Knucklehead to trickle out to a few carefully chosen riders for its final shakedown. It looked too good (placing the oil tank between motor and rear wheel was a masterstroke). It was too fast (it could top 90mph (145km/h) and was bristling with up-to-the-minute features. Apart from the engine, the old three-speed sliding gear transmission was ditched in favour of a modern four-speed constant mesh unit. Even the clutch, similar to the 45's, was

ABOVE
Although sidecars had been
priced out of the family market,
they were still popular among
enthusiasts.

OPPOSITE, ABOVE
The 45 may have had an
uncertain start, but it found a
niche in the Servi-Car.

OPPOSITE, BELOW
The 80ci VLH Big Twin ensured
Harley-Davidson always came
up with a strong answer to
Indian.

new. Harley-Davidson claimed 40hp at 4,800rpm (twice as much as the J) and it had a veritable hit: it had planned to make 1,600 61Es in 1936, but sold 1,926.

But despite their success, those early Knuckleheads vindicated Joe Petrali and upheld what was becoming a Harley-Davidson tradition – they had their troubles. Valve springs broke, oil pumps sometimes worked erratically and they kept on leaking oil. As with the VL and 45, a crash programme was instituted to rectify matters, and a change of spring supplier at least solved that problem. Troubled they certainly were (Harley-Davidson made 100 changes in the first year) but they mattered less with the Knucklehead than with the side-valves; they were less serious and not fundamental to the bike's design.

The Knucklehead did not just belatedly catch the competition, it leapt ahead, and it was easier to forgive foibles in a machine that was so far ahead in other ways. For the first time, Harley-Davidson had a technical lead over Indian, and it could be argued that the launch of the Knucklehead represented its final victory

over the Wigwam. Indian was never a serious threat to Harley after that, and as sales slowly recovered in the late thirties, Harley-Davidson's complete domination of the American motorcycle market was secured.

The founders had long been suspicious of racing and record-setting, but the Knucklehead's speed and power persuaded them that it was worth making a splash by attacking some mile speed records, records that were held by Indian. Hank Syvertson and Joe Petrali built up the record machine, and they made a lot of changes. There were twin carburettors, higher compression, and different cams and magneto, while a special high top gear of 3:1 was fitted to allow a theoretical top speed of 160mph (257km/h). It was all housed in a lightweight frame sporting an aerodynamic tail section and wheel discs, plus fairings for the forks and steering head.

As Petrali approached 100mph (161km/h) on the first run, the front wheel lifted and the bike went into a tank slapper. He was able to bring it to a halt but, rather than give up, ordered that all the aerodynamic bodywork be dumped.

Out again, on the naked machine, he attained 136.15mph (219.1km/h), and captured the record. It was all a bit disappointing though, only 10mph (16km/h) quicker than the previous record set by a slightly modified Indian made in 1924! Doubly disappointing for Petrali – Walter Davidson had promised him a $1,000 bonus if he reached 150mph (241km/h). Despite all the good publicity produced by the new record, Joe never got his bonus. But if there were any doubts concerning the Knucklehead's reliability, they were laid to rest the following month when a police officer named Fred Hamm rode a standard bike (albeit fitted with the latest valve gear-changes) through the 24-hour distance record. The course was a 5-mile (8-km) circle in the middle of dry Lake Muroc. Stopping only for fuel and fruit juice, Hamm rode round that circle continuously, covering 1,825 miles (2,937km) at an average 76.02mph/122.3km (which included stops). The chain was replaced at 1,400 miles (2,253km), but the Knucklehead itself ran perfectly. At last, Harley-Davidson had a bike that was both fast and reliable.

One sometimes gets the impression that the

four founders, practical to a man, scorned such things as product image and hype in general. But they lost no time in adapting the solid side-valves to capitalize on the Knucklehead's reflected glory, not to mention its engineering advances. The 45, 74 and 80 twins all received the new dry sump lubrication system (not before time either, as the total-loss system belonged to the pioneer generation) while the bigger ones had the Knucklehead's double-loop frame and tubular Springer forks. All three were restyled to look like replica Knuckleheads and the rounded, welded tank, streamlined instrument panel and mid-mounted oil tank transformed these solid plodders into thoroughly modern-looking motorcycles. They got new designations as well – the 45 was now the W-series, and the big twins were the U-series.

It was the right time to make the twins look a little snazzier. America's recovery continued and the customers had a little extra money to spend. In 1937, 90 per cent of them were opting for the standard or de luxe accessory packs, the latter providing Ride Control (instant adjustment of the Springer fork), front Safety Guard (forerunner of the modern crash bar), steering damper, fender light, side stand, stop light,

1937 was the year the VL (and the 45) finally received dry sump lubrication – and not before time either, as it is actually a 1938 bike, but still shows the Knucklehead styling which all the side-valve twins received the year before. Note the rounded tank with speedometer binnacle, central oil tank, and tubular Springer forks.

THEY'RE newer than new, hotter than hot, faster than fast, and neater than neat. These new 1934 model they're honeys! These new 1934 model Harley-Davidsons make previous models, as good as they were, look out of date, and no foolin'. These 1934 dream ships with their ultra-modern styling will make your old heart go pit-a-pat when you check them over. Boy, every time we look at a 1934 going over the 1934 speed chariots from stem to stern to find out what makes them the kind of a motorcycle you and I used to dream about. Here we go—hang on.

Streamlined Fenders on '34 Twins!
Look at these new fenders! Ain't that

DAVIDSON

1934

sumpin! Streamlining adapted to a motorcycle at its very best. Air-flo design is what we call it, and it matches up in style with the dynamite and wallop packed in these 1934 motors. Fenders that will give you greater protection than ever before. Fenders that spell class, with their smooth, clean sides, right down to the graceful sweep of the fender ends. And, man, oh man, look at that new diamond paneling on the fenders and tanks. Hot cha-cha, look at that new tank insignia—wings of speed, and boy! Enough

for those new fenders, which now make Harley-Davidsons the sleekest looking motorcycles ever offered to the riding public.

VLD Type Motors in All 74's

Let's go on and see more of this great new mile eater. We can't keep it back any longer, we've got to tell you now! All Big Twins will be of the same type as supplied in the VLD model of last year, and we don't have to tell you that these motors are good. When you pour in that throttle, these new 1934 VLD motors cut

New Oiler, TNT Motors, Stream-Lined Styling, New Color Designs, Air-flo Tail Light, New Aluminum Pistons, High-flo Tail Pipe.

coloured gearshift knob, rubbers for the foot pedals, saddlebags, and various pieces of chrome. The company learned early on that parts, accessories and clothing made far more profit than the motorcycles. That is why it still offers a massive aftermarket range of things to buy, and why many other current manufacturers have followed its example. Nonetheless, the thirties saw no return to the record sales of the previous decade: even the Knucklehead failed to make much practical difference to Harley-Davidson production, which fluctuated around 10,000 a year for the remainder of the decade.

What undoubtedly did make a difference to Harley-Davidson sales and profits was the famous Servi-Car. Not only was it a production engineer's dream (opening up a whole new market while sharing many of its components with current models) but it sold well, being suited to a multitude of uses. Milwaukee originally envisaged it as a useful tool for garages, enabling one driver to pick up and deliver customers' cars. But traffic police and meter maids loved its manoeuvrability (compared to that of a car) and ease of use. The rear track was designed to match the tracks of car tyres in mud or snow. Of course, with the 45's side-valve twin asked to pull even more weight

than in its motorcycle form, the Servi-Car was anything but fast. But it did keep going. Incredibly, it remained in production until 1974, still with that 45ci (734cc) V-twin providing the motive power. Apart from a similar device marketed by the inventive Alfred Rich Child in Japan (he persuaded the factory to supply some bikes with extra long chains and no rear wheel) the Servi-Car remained a uniquely American institution. In Europe, small car-based vans were favoured for making local deliveries, traffic police preferred solos, and the traditional sidecar held its own. As for the meter maids (traffic wardens in Britain) these unfortunates have always had to walk.

Late in the decade, two things happened which were minor milestones in the company's history. William Davidson died: the eldest brother

A 1937 Knucklehead from the first full year of production. Despite Harley-Davidson's determination to make it a limited production bike, demand took off, and so did Harley-Davidson's image.

Specifications

5, Model DL
Engine

Type	45-degree V-twin, side-valve
Bore x stroke	2.75 x 3.81in (70 x 97mm)
Capacity	45ci (746cc)
Compression ratio	5:1 (D 4:3, DLD 6:1)
Lubrication	Total loss
Power	18.5hp @ 4,000rpm (D 15hp, DLD 20hp)

Transmission

Clutch	Dry, fibre/metal discs
Gearbox	Three-speed, sliding gear
Final drive	Chain

Chassis

Frame	Tubular steel
Front suspension	Springer, leading link
Rear suspension	None
Front brake	Cable-operated drum
Rear brake	Drum
Tyres	3.85 x 25in (98 x 635mm)
Wheelbase	56.5in (144cm)
Fuel capacity	3.75 gallons (17 litres)

had been ill for some time, ignoring medical advice and continuing to indulge his generous appetite for food and strong German lager. Although less in the limelight than Arthur the salesman or Bill Harley the designer, it was William Davidson's tight control of production that maintained Milwaukee as a remarkably efficient factory. He was reputed to be paternal as well as firm, but the company had increased in size to such a degree that such a personal form of management was difficult to maintain. When, after the uncertainties of two slumps the workforce began to ask for unionization, Davidson resisted. But after his death, William Ottaway took over the production job and signed an agreement with the United Auto Workers, underlining the fact that Harley-Davidson had grown far from its small beginnings.

ABOVE
The R-series, known to all and sundry as the '45' and recognizable by the vertical dynamo which earned it the nickname 'three- cylinder Harley'.

LEFT
This late model two-tone VL has the Knucklehead styling and dry sump lubrication – also that massive sprung saddle, still mounted on a long spring inside the frame. In the days before rear suspension it was essential, and on good roads, perfectly adequate.

The 1940s:
Doing Well by Doing Good

**The hopeful 1940s – The ohv 45 – Early war trials – The WLA – Copying a BMW –
Mini-Jeeps and generator sets – The Panhead as evolution – The Hummer – Imports on the horizon**

The WLA introduced thousands of people to motorcycling in general and Harleys in particular.

A bigger 74ci engine was the only major Knucklehead change for the early forties.

Harley-Davidson emerged in the forties with renewed confidence. It had survived two slumps and many difficult years in between; it had bested its arch-rival and transformed itself from producers of tourist-fodder side-valves to something far more exciting: if you had just read the catalogues for 1940, you could be forgiven for thinking that Milwaukee was heading for a new decade of civilian prosperity.

For that year, the biggest twin had new

HARLEY–DAVIDSON
Motorcycling's Pace-setter for 1941

by Hap Hayes

BRILLIANTLY ENGINEERED FOR GREATER PERFORMANCE AND VALUE . . . . .

★ Centrifugally-Controlled Oil Pump on All Models ★ New Design Clutch on All Models ★ Improved Transmission on 45 Twins and Servi-Cars ★ Improved 45 Twin and Servi-Car Clutch Releasing Mechanism ★ New, Quiet Big Twin Muffler ★ Airplane-Style Speedometer Dial ★ Improved 45 Twin Brakes ★ Positive-Grip Hand Brake Lever ★ Redesigned Big Twin Clutch Foot Lever Assembly ★ Giant Air Cleaner ★ Oxide-Coated Piston Rings ★ Hardened Gear Shifter Levers ★ New 45 Twin Tool Box ★ New Front Wheel on Servi-Cars ★ Relocated Police Radio Carrier ★ Classy Summer Sport Shield ★ A New Model—The 74 OHV ★ Beautiful Color Options ★ Lower Prices on 61 OHV and 45 WLDR.

WELL—WELL—WELL! Here we are again folks. Howdy! Greetings! and hello — from your ol' boy friend Hap Hayes, the head-hunter—oops, (gotta cut down on those horror stories I've been reading) I mean headline hunter. And what a headline story I've got to tell. It's the hottest news story of the motorcycling year. So just bend your quivering ears in my direction while I give you all the interesting details on the 1941 line of Harley-Davidsons — the finest motorcycles I've

aluminium heads – lighter than the old cast-iron ones – and with over 40 per cent more cooling area: these were optional on the 74. The W-series 45 was not forgotten, being provided with the tubular Springer fork and an improved gear lever. And in WLD form it already had the ally heads. The following year saw the debut of the ohv 74ci (1200cc), either in response to police request, or to prevent civilian riders being overtaken by Indians, depending on who you believe. It also finally solved the old Knucklehead oil-pump problem of delivering too much lubrication to some parts, not enough to others. A centrifugally-controlled pump, with a bypass valve that closed at high revs, ensured maximum lubrication when the engine was working for its living. Not many 74 Knuckleheads reached civilian hands, though. Given the earlier 61ci (1000cc) problems, Harley-Davidson sensibly allowed only a trickle of 74s onto the market at first, to see how things went. A

few suffered from cracked crankcases, but thicker cases from 1941 cured all that. And of course, restrictions on wartime production got in the way; during hostilities only a few were built for essential services.

What with the success of the original Knucklehead, and the 74 in prospect, it is hardly surprising that the question of a 45ci (750cc) overhead valve twin came up more than once. The idea was not new and a bike had previously been built up using ohv parts from a hill-climb engine. The following year, Bill Harley and Bill Davidson's son (confusingly named William H. Davidson) advocated conversion of the existing 45 to ohv. Walter had favoured an all-new ohv 45, but he was persuaded by the cost argument as Harley was convinced the new bike could be built for the same price as the 74 side-valve. They went ahead and built a prototype (three were made eventually) building new heads and barrels

This was the last year of civilian production for a while, though to read the brochures you'd have thought Harley-Davidson was in business as usual. Instead, wartime restrictions left public demand on hold until 1946.

onto the existing 45 crankcase. In early 1939 it was taken on a 5,000-mile (8,047-km) round trip into Texas, along with a 74 ohv prototype. There were no apparent problems, and the engineering department began the work of cutting weight out of the bike. But soon after, other pressures on the R&D effort became apparent. Quite apart from the prospect of massive war work, there were improvements to the side-valves to work out, as well as the 74 ohv. The Board decided that it couldn't justify selling a sporting 45 for the same price as the big old side-valve, and the project

was dropped. It was nearly 20 years before Harley-Davidson finally made its 'small' ohv twin.

In retrospect, it is easy to see that the Board had more pressing matters on its mind. Although the United States wasn't yet at war, it was clear that tumultuous events across the Atlantic were beginning to concern them. The military had been planning for war, and in late 1938 Harley-Davidson received an initial order for 2,000 bikes from the Army. With an eye to much bigger business, a couple of W-series bikes were

A WLC belonging to Fred Warr who was an importer of Harleys into the U.K. The 'C' denotes that it is a Canadian version of the WL.

converted into the first WLAs (A for Army) and sent to Fort Knox for evaluation. They were up against an Indian V-twin and the Delco (really a BMW flat twin) but didn't come out too badly. The Harley was judged to have the best fording ability, but the military was most impressed with the BMW-Delco, with its shaft-drive, telescopic forks and generous ground clearance. Nor was it just interested in solo motorcycles. Before the advent of the Jeep, the Army had toyed with the idea of a motorcycle-based tricycle – one wheel at the front, two at the back, and shaft drive.

Harley-Davidson submitted a bid for this too, though Harley himself was convinced an enclosed chain would be at least as good as a shaft. He tried to convince the military as well, but it was set on shaft drive. Still, he was proved right when it came to smaller engines. The army was very keen to have a 30ci (492cc) bike. Indian obliged, but Harley refused to make it; according to one report, an official told him that if he persisted in refusing, ' ... you can consider yourself out of the motorcycle business'. It was an empty threat though, as on testing, Indian's small twin proved to be underpowered, and the idea was soon forgotten.

Meanwhile, the army liked the WLA enough to order 700 or so, in 1940. The WLA became one of Harley's milestone bikes, like the Knucklehead and first Evo. Familiar to a generation of servicemen (and not just Americans, for the WLA was used by all the allies), and countless war movie buffs, the wartime Harley has become an icon in itself. It transformed the 45's reputation as drab donkey to tough hero, and introduced thousands of people to motorcycling in general and Harleys in particular.

Unlike the F-model twins that headed for Europe in World War I, the WLA was extensively altered for its military role. There were actually several changes during production, but what follows is a typical specification. The V-twin came in low compression (5:1) form to give 23.5hp at 4,600rpm. There was a massive oil bath air filter and, with off-road running in mind, there

A trio of WLAs at a recent meet in Holland. Unlike the early twins that went to war on the Western Front, the WLA was highly modified for its military role.

was a skid plate, and two extra inches of ground clearance were obtained. The latter was evidently unsuccessful as it was dropped in 1942, and many earlier WLAs were converted back to standard forks. At the back, there was a more substantial luggage rack (the Army wanted to install a 40lb/18kg radio), the lights were to black-out specifications, and a gun scabbard ran parallel to the right fork to accommodate a rifle or a Thompson machine-gun. All this extra equipment dragged the WLA's performance even further down the scale, and top speed was round about 50mph (80km/h). But it was reliable, which out in the battlefield was rather more to the point.

A WLC for the Canadians had the brake and clutch levers reversed, and for some reason they did without the rear-view mirror. All military WLs had a metal plate on the tank, informing the rider of oil, spark plug and speed recommendations. Perhaps they were mindful of the fact that although thousands of riders were carefully trained by the military, while many others went through Harley-Davidson's own maintenance school, there would be many others who had done neither. The WLA survived them all to become the definitive U.S. Army bike. Nearly 90,000 were made during the war, and it is thought that there were enough spares to build another 30,000 on top of that. Most of all, its fundamental reliability gained it the respect of countless riders.

Such huge numbers make the WLA the most successful of all Harley-Davidson's military projects, but there were lots of these. Perhaps most significant was the XA. We have already seen how impressed the army was with the BMW layout of flat twin and shaft drive. As this was what it had insisted upon, Bill Harley obtained a BMW from preoccupation Holland and the resulting XA looked very similar, apart from the Springer forks; in fact, it was a straight copy. The side-valve 45ci (737cc) flat twin had square bore and stroke dimensions, two-throw crank and a single camshaft. It was said to run cooler than the WLA, thanks to the cylinders sticking out in the breeze, and lubrication was by wet sump. It was also, by the way, the first Harley-Davidson to have a hand-operated clutch. The army ordered 1,000 XAs which were built at great expense, the cost of tooling being spread over a small production run, though it is interesting that Harley-Davidson made sure to word the contract

so that it could use the XA tooling for commercial (i.e. civilian) products after six years had elapsed. A prototype XA with telescopic forks and ohv did indeed undergo extensive testing in 1946, but never made it to production. Maybe if it had we would now be celebrating the first half-century of the 'modern' flat twin Harleys. But in reality, the XA was doomed to a short military life caused by the event of the Jeep, which was able to do most of what a motorcycle and sidecar did in the battlefield, and much of the solo work besides.

There were plenty of other wartime projects that failed to achieve even the XA's limited production numbers. The Canadians required a power unit, probably for a remote-control mini-minesweeper, and Milwaukee obligingly built it up using two Knucklehead 61s. It apparently didn't do too well in testing, and no more was heard of it. The XA motorcycle may not have been a huge hit, but its flat twin engine was considered for all sorts of uses though four XA-powered snow sledges were built which apparently came to nothing. More promising was the 1,000lb (454kg) mini-Jeep. To be built by Willys, it was designed to be light enough to parachute onto the battlefield and was powered by a 49ci (803cc) ohv fan-cooled version of the flat twin, coupled to a three-speed gearbox. The WAC, as it was known, did well in testing, but in the end Willys was too busy building full-sized Jeeps to have time for it. Then there was the generator set – also using an ohv XA – of which the air force ordered nearly 5,000 in June 1945. Then the war ended and all contracts were unceremoniously cancelled.

Fortunately, Milwaukee had been planning its post-war line-up for some time. It looked as though an XA Servi-Car was certain, though in the event it never got beyond the prototype stage. Harley-Davidson certainly needed to plan for the future: Walter Davidson had died, aged 66, in February 1942, and Bill Harley the following year. There was speculation that Arthur, as sole remaining founder, would assume the company presidency, but the second generation was already well established and Bill Davidson's son William took up the helm. The engineering side remained part of the Harley dynasty; after a short period of tenure by the long-serving William Ottaway, the chief engineer's post went to Harley's son. Perhaps, after all the company had been through,

OPPOSITE, ABOVE
A rare machine, the 1948 Panhead had Springer forks, but went over to hydraulics the following year. Spotlights and saddlebags are period extras.

OPPOSITE, BELOW
The Panhead was Harley-Davidson's first engine to have hydraulic tappets.

Harley's first bike with telescopic forks. It was also the first to be given an official name — the Hydra-Glide. There was no rear suspension yet (that was still years away), but in any case, many long-time Harley riders were quite happy enough with the sprung seat post and large, squashy rear tyre.

there was a reluctance to bring in new blood from outside the two families. Harley-Davidson was certainly established as a family-run organization, and whether that did it any good in the long-term is questionable.

The new leadership certainly had its own problems to face. There was a huge pent-up demand for motorcycles in the years immediately following the war. Not only had the conflict introduced many to motorcycles for the first time,

but fuel had been rationed and the speed limit cut – at one time the ration was two gallons (9 litres) a week and the speed limit 35mph (56km/h). Now it was time to break free. Harley-Davidson's problem, together with the United States and the

rest of the world's industry, was material shortages. Under the Marshall Plan, some raw materials were being sent straight to Europe, and home supplies were strictly rationed. So plans for the XA-powered solo and Servi-Cars were

After its wartime glories, the WL returned to civilian life and endured until 1952. Although the 45 side-valve twin survived in the Servi-Car right up to the 1970s, it was by now thoroughly outdated, outrun by the far smaller British imports.

shelved, and the pre-war line-up reverted straight back into production. In any case, it could hardly complain – Harley-Davidson's dominance of the domestic industry is illustrated by the 1946 production figures: of 19,500 bikes built that year, three out of four was a Harley-Davidson.

Not that there was any room for complacency. For the first time, significant numbers of imported bikes were trickling into the North American market, specifically British bikes such as the Triumph, Velocette and Norton. These little 350s and 500s may not have had the stamina of a big V-twin, but they were quick and nimble. G.I.s stationed in Britain had been introduced to them, and they found a small but rapidly growing market in the United States. It is interesting to contrast the response of Indian and Harley-Davidson to this perceived threat. Indian decided to meet the opposition head-on, spending much of its now meagre resources on developing a 13ci (220cc) single and 27ci (440cc) vertical twin. The little Indians were mechanical disasters and all but ruined their parent company. But in Milwaukee, although an up-to-the-minute vertical twin was discussed at Board level (hydraulic forks, rear suspension, hand clutch/foot gearchange), it never got as far as a prototype.

Instead, Harley-Davidson determined to continue making what it knew best – big V-twins – and to gradually refine them as the years went on. You could call this either short-sighted or sensible, but for better or worse it took the company through those difficult post-war years. So after a couple of years of what was basically the pre-war Knucklehead with a few detail changes, came the Panhead. It certainly looked promising – aluminium heads for cooler running and hydraulic tappets for quieter performance. It looked like a classic refinement of a respected design as the changes promised a cure for the Knucklehead's occasional overheating and top-end oil leaks.

But it would not have been a true Harley-Davidson launch without some sort of trauma. The problem was the new tappets whose oil had to be pumped up from the base of the engine through a cat's cradle of oilways. The pump couldn't cope, and the resultant fluctuating oil pressure upset the valve timing, while rocker breakages were not unknown. In a now familiar post-launch phase, the factory rushed out a kit of parts to cure the problem. But other than that, the Panhead (so-called because of the saucepan-shaped rocker covers) was a genuine improvement. It was improved the following year when Bill Harley's 1907 Springer fork was finally dropped in favour of telescopics and the Hydra-Glide (the first in a long line of 'glides') was born. Inevitably, after 40 years there were some diehard enthusiasts who baulked at such new-fangled ideas, but the long-travel soft forks undeniably improved comfort. And they fitted right in with Harley tradition, with their own special teething troubles: early vented examples could spray their riders with oil, the long, soft action sometimes allowed the machine to ground out on tight turns and some complained that the telescopics lacked the precise steering of the Springer. In any case, the old sprung seat-post was still there, as were the fat, low-pressure tyres, and gear-change was still by hand. However, there remained much for which the traditionalists could be thankful.

There was an exception to this conservative policy – the S-125 – or the Hummer, as it was later known. It wasn't really new at all, but a pre-war DKW two-stroke, whose design was handed to the allies as part of wartime reparations. BSA called it the Bantam and went on making it for 25 years though Harley-Davidson made it for rather less. The little bike was simple in the extreme, having a pre-mix two-stroke with an alleged 3hp, a three-speed gearbox and rubber-band suspension. But it was actually quite a success, at least at first. William H. Davidson told his fellow directors that 10,000 of them were sold in the first seven months of 1947. If true, the 125 outsold the big twins that year. Being a pre-existing design, the little bike was almost devoid of troubles and the only real problem was that some Harley dealers refused to sell what they saw as a pipsqueak that didn't deserve to be called a motorcycle. Neither did it maintain the early success at a time when the public was ready to buy anything on wheels. In the late fifties, the Hummer, by now in 10ci (165cc) form with telescopic forks, sold only around 3,000 each year. It was finally dropped when Milwaukee's agreement with Aermacchi made it redundant.

Still, the company did keep a traditional firm hand with dealers to protect the 125. Many were selling the Cushman scooter as a sideline to the twin, but in the run-up to the new bike's launch were instructed to cease selling scooters

Specifications

1941 WLA
Engine

Type	Air-cooled V-twin, side-valve
Capacity	45ci (746cc)
Bore x stroke	2.75 x 3.81in (70 x 97mm)
Compression ratio	5:1
Power	$23\frac{1}{2}$bhp @ 4,600rpm

Transmission

Gearbox	Three-speed
Final drive	Chain

Chassis

Frame	Tubular steel
Front suspension	Springer leading link fork
Rear suspension	None
Front brake	Cable-operated drum
Rear brake	Drum
Tyres	4.00 x 18in (102 x 457mm)
Wheelbase	59.5in (151cm)
Fuel capacity	3.4 gallons (15 litres)
Top speed	65mph (105km/h)
Fuel consumption	c. 35mpg (12km per litre)

It was always a measure of the yawning gap between the American and European industries that the WL was a 750cc heavyweight monster by British standards, but the 'baby' of the Harley-Davidson range.

forthwith. To refuse meant that they would have no more twins to sell, which would effectively destroy their business. In other words, Harley-Davidson was flexing its muscles a little, using its near monopoly of a certain type of bike to exert its will. Then there were the racing rules of the AMA (American Motorcycle Association). It could be argued that the little British bikes were not in direct competition with the twins and were actually doing some good by attracting new riders to the sport. However, some Harley dealers had abandoned Milwaukee to sell the imports and (worse) the 45 WR racer faced humiliation on the race track. But despite protests from the importers, the AMA (now dominated by Harley-

Davidson) upheld the compression rule – 31ci (500cc) ohv singles had to not only compete against the 45ci (750cc) side-valves, but were limited to a 7.5:1 compression ratio, which almost obliterated their power advantage.

So, as the war drew to a close, Harley-Davidson had much to be optimistic about. Indian was all but defunct (it finally succumbed in 1953), it had invested $3.5 million in new plant and tooling, and the big twins were as popular as ever, and updated. And while those English imports might be selling well (and some dealers were certainly clamouring for a middleweight Harley-Davidson to match them) they were attracting new riders who, in the fullness of time, would progress to proper, full-sized motorcycles. Funnily enough, the moribund British industry was to console itself 20 years later in exactly the same way, when the Japanese began to make their presence felt.

Specifications

1949 Hydra-Glide Panhead
Engine

Type	Air-cooled V-twin, ohv, hydraulic tappets
Capacity	74ci (1200cc)
Bore x stroke	3.43 x 3.97in (87 x 101mm)
Lubrication	Dry sump
Power	50hbp @ 4,800rpm

Transmission

Primary drive	Chain
Gearbox	Four-speed, hand-change
Final drive	Chain

Chassis

Frame	Tubular steel
Front suspension	Hydraglide hydraulic forks
Rear suspension	None
Front brake	Cable-operated 8in (20cm)drum
Rear brake	8in (20cm) drum
Tyres	5.00 x 16in (127 x 406mm)
Wheelbase	59.5in (151cm)
Fuel capacity	3.75 gallons (17 litres)
Weight (dry)	560lb (254kg)

Chapter Six
The 1950s:
From Mainstream to Niche Market

Imports flourish and dealers flex their muscles – Old wine, new bottle (the K-series) – The Duo Glide – Bobbing and the customizers – The other milestone, the Sportster

Harley-Davidson's dirty linen was being washed in public, and from then on things would never be quite the same.

Harleys came to be seen as outdated dinosaurs in the first decade or two after the war when, compared to the new imports, English or Japanese, they appeared crude and overweight and as though technical development had somehow passed them by. But looking more closely at the gradual updates made to the big twins after the war, a different picture emerges: aluminium heads and hydraulic tappets in 1948 and telescopic forks in 1949 (just as the British bikes were adopting them). Harley might have been a bit late with foot shifting (1952) and rear suspension (1958), but not disastrously so, while

The K-series was an odd mixture of old and new – unit construction, up-to-date chassis, but with an underpowered side-valve twin.

12-volt electrics (1964) and electric start (1965) came well before any of the British factories adopted them.

None of which made the big twins acceptable to the new breed of sports bikers. Harley-Davidsons were still a product of the American market, pure and simple, a fact well illustrated by the proportion that were exported in the mid-sixties – a mere 3 per cent! But despite all that (or perhaps because of it) the big Harleys went on selling steadily in America. While it is true that sales fell in the early fifties (from a best-ever peak of over 30,000 in 1948) they recovered steadily from 1956. The FL bikes hovered around 5–6,000 a year throughout, then rose again in the sixties. Market share fell, because the U.S. motorcycle market as a whole was expanding, but Milwaukee was keeping hold of its traditional club and touring riders. In short, the big twin was shifting from mainstream to niche market.

With hindsight, this is obvious: but all that Harley-Davidson could see was that, as the new decade dawned, imports had grabbed 40 per cent of the U.S. market. They decided to petition the White House to slap a 40 per cent tariff on imported bikes, and a quota system for imports based on pre-war figures – in other words, virtually zero! It was not a good move. Over a three-week hearing, the importers of BSAs and Triumphs vigorously defended their right to supply a free market; the Tariff Commission agreed, and rejected Harley-Davidson's submission. That was bad enough, but the evidence at this public hearing revealed several unpalatable facts. BSA importer Alfred Rich Child (the same who had previously pioneered Harley-Davidson exports to Africa and the Far

East) told of Harley's restrictive controls on its dealers and its opposition to allowing a market for smaller bikes to develop. So Harley-Davidson's dirty linen was being washed in public, and things were never quite the same again.

It certainly gave the dealers new heart, realizing that they could take on other franchises and there wasn't much Milwaukee could do about it and Skip Fordyce, a long-serving Harley dealer in Riverside, California, began to sell Triumphs as well. When warned by the company that his old franchise could be revoked, Fordyce simply replied that he would take the company to court, citing the anti-trust laws. Harley-Davidson backed down in what has been described as a landmark case, and many other Harley-Davidson dealers at last discovered that they were free to sell whatever they liked. All in all, it was not a good year: right at the end of 1950, the last surviving founder, Arthur Davidson, was killed in a car crash. The death of the man who had done so much to inaugurate and develop the company would, in most circumstances, have meant a

change of direction. But the founders' sons were already well in control of Harley-Davidson and, for a while, little would be changing.

This was underlined by the K-series, which superseded the old 45ci W in 1952. Although some dealers had taken on import franchises, there were others who would much rather have had a home-grown bike to counter the imports. According to Milwaukee, the K was the motorcycle they had been waiting for. And if you looked at the chassis design, that's exactly what it was. The K was bang up-to-date, with telescopic forks, swinging-arm rear-end, unit construction and foot-shift. Unfortunately, that was as far as it went, for the K-series used a development of the old side-valve 45ci twin that had been around since the twenties. It is also something of a moot point as to how much was new and how much was carried over: it was 'identical' (Sucher), 'revamped' (Wright), 'all-new' (Bolfert). Whichever of these Harley historians you agree with (and the new engine's bore and stroke were identical to the old ones),

The styling of the K-bike was up-to-date, in a cobby sort of way, but without the elegance of a Triumph twin.

Harley's long-running WR racer was superseded by the KR. Both bikes had unpromising starts, yet were gradually developed into competitive machines.

there is no getting away from the fact that, with side-valves and not a great deal of power, it was no match for any of the imports.

The outsider may be mystified as to why Harley-Davidson stuck with this outmoded layout when it had spent so much time and effort changing everything else about the K. It wasn't as though an overhead valve 45 was a radical concept within the company – Bill Harley had been arguing the case for one in 1939. William H. Davidson was later to say that the K was just a stopgap model to maintain the status quo until an ohv bike appeared. But it was on the market for four years, long enough for a new bike to be developed. That all-new bike existed, and the KL was an all-aluminium 60-degree V-twin with ohv, twin carburettors and high cams; it reached the prototype stage, but not production. And when the ohv replacement did finally go on sale, it was the much less radical Sportster.

All this happened behind the scenes. The reality for Harley-Davidson dealers was a bike that looked up-to-date but which could barely exceed 80mph (129km/h) when the Triumph Thunderbird could top 100. This was not enough. Sales were disappointing, and Harley-Davidson responded after a couple of years with the bigger 55ci (900cc) K. In high compression KK form this could be coaxed to do over 90mph, but it was still no Thunderbird beater. There was also a competition KR to take over from the WR, but here too the early results were disappointing. It produced less power than the 1941 WR, and the full-suspension handling was not as good. On the other hand, its foot-shifting four-speed gearbox was a real improvement and veteran tuners, such as Tom Sifton, were later able to coax more power out of the side-valve.

Meanwhile, the bigger twins were not being neglected. The same year the K was introduced, the FL acquired a foot gearchange and hand clutch – a marked departure from tradition. If you really insisted, you could still have a foot clutch and handchange, but that really illustrated the highly conservative nature of both the company and the traditional market it served. For any of the British or European factories to have produced a hand gearchange in the 1950s would have been considered laughable. The hydraulic tappets were improved as well, being moved from the top to the base of the pushrods, which made them less vulnerable to oil-pressure fluctuations as well as reducing top-end oil leaks. And thanks to different cams and improved porting, power was up by 10 per cent.

To repeat, the big twins were being transformed from mainstream to niche products. If anything, the result was their riders becoming more conservative rather than less, and buying a big, heavy twin now needed a positive decision rather than acceptance of what was merely available. Perhaps this was why the Duo Glide of 1958, with its swinging-arm rear suspension, failed to receive a universal welcome. Not only did it add a massive 80lb (36kg) to the weight of the FL, but many riders considered that the old sprung seat-post (a Harley-Davidson feature almost since the two-men-and-a-shed days), and big, low-pressure tyres made it superfluous. In fitting rear suspension, Harley-Davidson was

doing no more than following an inevitable trend, but not everyone wanted it. Soon, hardtail replacement frames were on sale, though the Duo Glide was here to stay.

In fact, those hardtail frames were the manifestation of the nascent custom movement. Bikes in general, and Harleys in particular, had been modified by their riders for years, but there was something different about the new wave of stripped-down Harleys that were beginning to emerge from California. This first came to public attention when Hollister leaped into the headlines back in 1947, where a supposed 'riot' between visiting bikers and the locals is said to have occurred. Harley-Davidson and the AMA rapidly distanced themselves from gangs with names such as Satan's Sinners. For them, motorcycling was a healthy outdoor activity, pursued by respectable, clean-cut men and women. For groups like Satan's Sinners, motorcycling was at the centre of a lifestyle which rejected the mainstream altogether. Their bikes reflected that and were invariably Harley-Davidson big twins with every piece of superfluous equipment torn off to reduce weight and increase performance. This was the advent of the 'California Bobber' and the birth of the modern custom movement. It is odd that, while Harley-Davidson distanced itself from these early outlaws, it has since embraced a highly stylized version of what they

The K-series, in fact, went on to race well into the sixties, aided by AMA rules which allowed side-valve machines a capacity advantage. It was not until 1970 that Harley-Davidson finally announced its ohv racer, the XR750. After a shaky start, this too came to dominate the ovals.

set out to achieve, and virtually made it its own, while nowadays the so-called outlaws thumb their nose at bourgeois convention at weekends, reverting to respectability for the remainder of the time.

But while big twin riders divided themselves into outlaws and tourists, a third group was still beyond the company's grasp. Riders of Triumphs and Nortons just could not take the K model seriously, and in 1957 Harley-Davidson finally gave them a real alternative. It was the Sportster, as much a milestone bike as

the Knucklehead had been 20 years earlier. With overhead valves and a 7.5:1 compression, the 55ci (or 883cc, the classic Sportster capacity) produced 40hp at 5,500rpm. This was enough to equal the British 650 twins but not surpass them, so in 1958 the higher compression XLH appeared, with bigger valves and smoothed-out ports. The year after that, power was up again, to 55hp at 6,800rpm. Here once more was a Harley that could stay with any other contemporary bike, though it still wasn't as nimble as the lighter imports.

The year 1958, and the Duo Glide finally brings swinging-arm rear suspension to the big twin, even though it was not universally welcomed.

The other thing it gained that year was that classic look we associate with the Sportster – the small tank and staggered pipes which came in with the XLCH. Its origins lay in the 1958-only XLC. A group of Californian dealers had persuaded Milwaukee to supply them with a stripped-down Sportster (no lights or battery, and magneto ignition) and just 200 were produced. The XLCH was a canny attempt to cash in on the XLC's competition looks. Nominally intended as a competition-oriented version (hence the higher pipes, magneto ignition and semi-knobbly tyres),

the important thing about the XLCH (CH = 'Competition Hot', allegedly) was not how it went but how it looked. That classic fuel tank came off none other than the little 7.6ci (125cc) Hummer. Holding just 2.2 gallons (10 litres) of fuel, it may not have taken you very far, but it set off the 'small' V-twin to a tee. It was well complemented by a small headlamp and those staggered pipes. With a couple of new colours the Sportster was transformed from a dumpy mini-tourer (hard to believe now that the Sportster could once be specified with screen and panniers) into the lean all-engine machine that endeared it to thousands. It outsold the standard bike by two to one.

Not that the Sportster was a huge and instant hit. It was outsold by the big twins right through to 1969 and it was not until the seventies that it was a major part of the Harley-Davidson line-up; until 1964, less than one in five Harley sales was a Sportster. But that was unimportant. What did matter was that the Sportster had opened (or more accurately re-opened) a new market for Milwaukee and was providing sports bikers with a viable alternative to the imports.

But Harley-Davidson still had no small bikes on offer. This was not such a great problem when British bikes were the main imports (they had progressed from 350 singles to 500 and 650 twins) but Japanese bikes were starting to appear

Telescopic forks in 1949, rear in 1958, electric start in 1965. Gradually, very gradually, the big touring Harley was beginning to evolve. But fundamentally it was too heavy and unwieldy to have mainstream appeal.

RIGHT
The Panhead remained the standard Harley twin through to 1965 – its 17-year lifespan being far from untypical.

BELOW
The Sportster – the bike which did every bit as much for Harley-Davidson as the original Knucklehead.

FAR RIGHT, ABOVE
Occasionally, the British motorcycling press would sample a Harley, amazed at its comfort while regarding it as hardly suitable for twisty English 'B' roads.

BELOW
It was interesting that in 1958 Harley-Davidson still portrayed the typical rider as a clean-cut sportsman; this was, by now, out of step with the public's perception of bikers of the time.

on the horizon, while the 10ci (165cc) Hummer was getting on in years. The trouble was, Harley-Davidson was short of money, and hence development funds. It made modest profits throughout the fifties, but much of these were frittered away in handsome dividends to its shareholders. It considered diversification but the central fact remained; Harley-Davidson needed a lightweight motorcycle. In June 1959, the Development Committee recommended that the best way to achieve this was to import someone else's bike and stick a Harley-Davidson badge on it and that is in fact what happened.

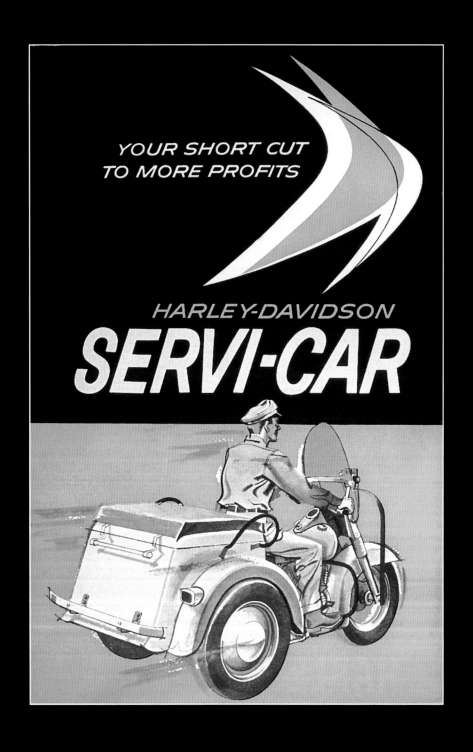

Chapter Seven
The 1960s:
Selling Up, Selling Out

**Buying Aermacchi – The Sprint and tiddlers – the Sportster grows up – KR, XR750 –
The Shovelhead and Electra Glide – Going public – Selling up**

The big twins sold well to American riders but had little relevance to anyone else.

It was in the summer of 1960 that Harley-Davidson entered negotiations with Aermacchi, a motorcycle maker based in Varese, Italy. The Italians made a range of small bikes but were struggling to keep their heads above water. Harley-Davidson needed a small bike to sell but did not have the time or the money to develop one of its own. The negotiations were predictably swift and it wasn't long before Harley-Davidson bought a 50 per cent interest in the firm.

Aermacchi's origins was as a manufacturer of aircraft whose plant had been destroyed during the war. It turned to scooters after the defeat of the Axis powers and followed this up, in 1956, with a 175 or 250 four-stroke single named the Chimera. Like Moto Guzzi's Falcone, this placed the cylinder almost horizontal, and gave the little bike its distinctive appearance. An 80mph (129km/h) sports version of the 250 appeared in 1957, and was by all accounts a fine handling bike, thanks in part to the low centre of gravity provided by that low-set cylinder. New skimpier mudguards, a smaller tank and new name (the Sprint) turned it into a Harley-Davidson and the company began to import them in 1961.

It was not the ideal solution as the Sprint was half a class down from the British 500s, but it fitted neatly into Harley-Davidson's range above the home-grown two-strokes, and a 350 version was to follow later in the decade. Also, the British 250s were nothing like as successful as their bigger bikes in America, so there was room for the Sprint to do well. *Cycle World* tested one in early 1962, praising its power and torque – it would pull strongly to 7,500rpm –

loved the handling, and pronounced it capable of cruising at 65–70mph (105–113km/h). It has to be said that there was nothing very high-tech about the Sprint; its pushrod engine and kickstart would be overtaken by the Japanese in a few years' time, but for Harley it provided instant access to a growing market. Not everyone at Milwaukee was to be quite so enthusiastic about Varese and its products over the coming years, quite apart from the logistics of co-ordinating two factories thousands of miles apart, and it became clear that Italian electrics and finish were not up to traditional Harley standards.

Meanwhile, Harley-Davidson's own little bikes were updated to back up the new imports. The little 7.6ci (125cc) Hummer had already acquired a 10ci (165cc) engine and telescopic forks. Now it became the Pacer 175 in road form. As the Scat, it was a dual-purpose bike with high-level exhaust and front mudguard, plus knobbly tyres; trail bikes (or street scramblers, as they were known) were the coming thing, and a Sprint trail bike appeared the year after. The Ranger was the pure off-roader, with no lights or front 'guard, higher ground clearance and lower gearing. All three shared that elderly two-stroke and a basic frame without rear suspension and when the Japanese lightweights arrived, Harley's own little bikes were revealed as crude and outdated. They were dropped in 1966.

But Harley-Davidson was certainly making a determined assault on the small bike market. The Topper scooter appeared in 1960, just as the first overtures were being made to Aermacchi. Using the 10ci (165cc) engine, it came in restricted 5hp AU form, or the no-holds-barred 9hp A. The essentials were there: it was mechanically simple and offered weather protection and fully automatic transmission. Unfortunately, it was also too heavy for the little two-stroke and at $600 cost more than the Japanese opposition. And quite apart from anything else, its square-rigged lines had nothing like the style of a classic Vespa or Lambretta. Despite encouraging sales in its first year (Milwaukee made over 3,800), and a cameo role in a popular TV series, the Topper failed to do well, and quietly made its exit in 1964.

But if Harley-Davidson's home-built tiddlers weren't setting the world on fire, the Sportster was a different matter. Since its first couple of power upgrades, the 'little' twin was proving as quick in a straight line, if not quicker, as any bike then in production. Local hot-shots would meet on a Saturday night to debate what became the eternal question throughout most of the sixties – which was fastest off the line, a Sportster or a Triumph/Norton/BSA twin? A horsepower race ensued: just as Milwaukee had rapidly endowed the Sportster with more power, so Triumph introduced its legendary Bonneville in 1962, while Norton was to up its twin to 46ci (750cc).

For the first time in quite a while, Harley-Davidson was facing direct competition, and it did it no harm. By the mid-sixties, even the 'touring' XLH was a mildly hot motorcycle, with its 9:1 compression and 55hp at 6,300rpm. It could run the standing quarter in 15.5 seconds

and only just failed to crack 100mph (161km/h). Mind you, the standard XLH was still a dumpy-looking object. With its big tank and headlamp nacelle – not to mention the optional screen and panniers – it was worlds away from the Sportster look now familiar to all. It was a heavy old beast too, at 505lb (229kg), 100lb more than the opposition. Perhaps it was the weight that drove *Cycle World* to comment that a 1965 Sportster, 'gives the impression that it is designed to be held more or less vertical, and steered by aiming the front wheel – like an automobile'.

Better was to come: within three years the XLH had acquired that classic tank, extra power (58bhp at 6,800rpm) and could top a genuine 114mph (183km/h) while the standing quarter took 13.8 seconds. With its electric start, it weighed more than ever, though newer superbikes like the BSA/Triumph threes and Honda fours were putting on the pounds as well. And according to *Cycle World*, it now handled properly, as well. Perhaps it was the new forks which appeared in 1968, but whatever the reason, the magazine appeared to be discussing a completely different motorcycle to that mini-touring '65. Words like 'precision', and phrases such as 'builds rider confidence' and 'seat-of-the-pants rider awareness' cropped up. It was difficult to remember a time when any Harley received praise for the way it went round corners. The only apparent downside was the drum brakes

The Topper (seen here with a peculiar sidecar attachment) was Harley's answer to the Italian motor scooter that was so popular in Europe. But, like the BSA/Triumph scooters of the sixties, the Topper lacked the style of a Vespa and the affordability of a Honda. As the sixties ended, Harley-Davidson at last got the message – 'Do what you do best!'

which could overheat and fade (discs were still five years away) and the 2.2-gallon (10-litre) tank which might look good, but you had to think about fuel every 80 miles (129km) or so.

In fact, the late sixties was perhaps the Sportster's golden age. As other big bikes got heavier, it no longer seemed overweight, and it was their equal in speed. It even offered electric start, which the British triples did not. It is tempting to look at the Sportster's evolution and conclude that it kept Harley-Davidson afloat throughout that period. On the other hand, despite its high profile, the Sportster was being outsold by the big twins right up to 1968. As Harley-Davidson's range proliferated, the XL series found itself a fairly minor player. Even in its impactful first year, Sportsters made up only 18 per cent of Milwaukee's output, and retained around that share up until 1968, when sales finally began to take off. Even during its seventies' sales peak, the XL could only manage one in three Harley sales. By then though, it was established enough to have its own faithful followers and Sportster riders became just as

loyal as the big twin *afficionados*.

Meanwhile, how were the Italian imports doing? Oddly enough, as the decade wore on and competition got fiercer, the Sprint sold better and better. It went slowly at first – less than 1,700 in its first full year and 1,900 the year after. At least some of the quality problems were actually not Aermacchi's fault; it made the engine itself (which was mechanically very reliable) but bought everything else in, including those troublesome electrics. So Milwaukee engineers, attempting to keep track of the problems, were not only having to liaise with one Italian factory, but several.

But it was not all bad news. Harley and Aermacchi proved willing to launch variations on the Sprint theme, as well as increasing power year on year. The CRS of 1966, for example, was a no-holds-barred scrambles version. Sold without lights or speedometer, its high compression (10.0:1) version of the 250 single produced 28bhp at 8,500rpm and, remarkably for an undersquare pushrod engine, it could rev to 9,500 without damage. In racing CR-TT form it

A police Servi-Car, 1960 version. That adaptable old side-valve 45 had powered racers, custom bikes, tourers and sidecar outfits; but the Servi-Car remained its most enduring application.

could manage 35bhp at 10,000. The various competition Sprints did well in private hands and a streamlined Sprint reached 176mph (283km/h) on the Bonneville flats, thus securing the world 15ci (250cc) speed record for Milwaukee and boosting Sprint sales which rocketed to 3,000 that same year, to over 5,000 in 1966 and to 9,000 the following year.

But the 250 single had really reached the limit of its development and Harley-Davidson/Aermacchi responded with the SS350 in 1969. They claimed only 25bhp for this one, though it was in a less frenetic state of tune than the last 250s, and could in any case still exceed 90mph (145km/h). The magazines liked it; despite its basic age, the Sprint was still a good handler and fun to ride. True, most of the Japanese opposition (especially the two-strokes) were faster and more flashy, and when all was said and done, this was basically a 12-year-old pushrod single with kickstart and four-speed

gearbox. But it went on selling a steady 4–4,500 each year, right up until 1974.

Not that it was alone any longer. In the middle of the sixties, Harley had started to import Aermacchi two-stroke mopeds alongside the Sprint. The M-50 made quite a good impression: it was cheap enough, with proper rear suspension and reasonable quality. It is difficult to believe now, but Harley-Davidson's best-selling bike in both 1965 and 1966 was this 3ci (50cc) moped, with over 16,000 of them leaving the showroom floor in that second year. Then it upped the capacity to 4ci (65cc), launched a big advertising campaign ('62 per cent more horsepower ... a barrel of fun for everyone') and the whole idea seemed to fall flat. The 65cc Harley never matched the popularity of the 50.

With ohv firmly established on Harley-Davidson road bikes, it seems odd that most efforts in competitions of the early to mid-sixties were concentrated on the side-valve KR. The

while large valves and careful cam design ensured a decent power output across a broad rev range. The rules would have to be changed, and when Harley-Davidson approached them the AMA happily responded. (It had already instigated a new 250 class to suit the Sprint at Harley's behest.) With rules to suit, the XR750 hit the dirt tracks, though its first year was not a happy one. Not until the original iron barrels were replaced with aluminium ones the following season did it start to come good. And when it did, the XR proceeded to dominate American dirt track racing for the next two decades. It even managed some road race wins in its early years before, like the big British twins, it was outclassed by the new breed of Japanese two-strokes. As with the KR (not to mention the WR before that) the XR succeeded through continuous development; those early iron-barrelled engines produced only 70bhp, but the aluminium barrels allowed cooler running and a higher compression with 90bhp the eventual result.

If Harley's race bikes were a triumph of development over design, the same could be said of the big twins, the 74ci (1200cc) Panhead and Shovelhead. They hardly changed in the early sixties; Harley-Davidson had its hands full with the new Aermacchi tiddlers, and work on the big bikes was limited to a new rear-chain oiler and external oil lines. But in 1964 came a taste of things to come when 12-volt electrics came along. The reason became clear the following year with what was to be one of motorcycling's all-time classic model names – the Electra Glide. Electra Glide is often referred to in hushed tones as a unique and special model, but the Electra was no more nor less than the standard FLH with an electric starter. It would not have been a Harley launch without a modicum of drama, and the first starter obliged by a susceptibility to shorting out in wet weather, which was ironic, as the system had been developed to service outboard marine engines! A new system from the Homelight Corporation was rapidly substituted and all was well. Mind you, with bigger battery and all the accoutrements, it added a massive 75lb (34kg) to the FLH's weight.

To cope, power was increased, but the big news engine-wise came in 1966 when the 20-year-old Panhead was finally updated. The Shovelhead (not an official Harley name, as none

OPPOSITE
Duo Glide, 1961. This was a quiet time for the big twin, with Harley-Davidson preoccupied with Aermacchi and Sportster derivatives. Parts of this bike are reminiscent of a Heritage Softail, others of a Fat Boy, the fifties and sixties being periods Harley turned to good account with its nostalgic, retro bikes.

KR, you may remember, was the disappointing racer version of the road-going K, whose *raison d'être* were the long-running AMA competition rules which favoured side-valve V-twins. Ten years on, the KR had benefited from on-going development (notably from independent tuners as well as Harley-Davidson itself), just like its predecessor, the WR. As a result, it kept on winning races – 18 wins in 23 national races in 1968, when Cal Rayborn made the first 100mph (161km/h) lap at Daytona, KR-mounted. Of course, cynics would say that the KR's success was due as much to the AMA's side-valve-biased rules and the fact that there were simply so many of them. Still, it cannot be denied that the later KR was a real triumph of development over design.

Milwaukee knew this couldn't last forever though, and came up with the XR750 to replace the KR. This used a sleeved-down Sportster engine to produce an ohv twin of 45ci (750cc),

just what was needed for crossing the continent fully laden. It could very nearly reach 100mph (161km/h), and would rumble along all day at 60–70 on its tall gearing. Everyone agreed that the new engine was a great improvement, and the only real drawback was the brakes. As the opposition were going over to modern discs, Harley stuck with a hydraulic drum at the back and a cable-operated drum on the front, hardly changed since the first Panhead. One could forgive the Electra Glide many things, but the inability to stop a 783lb (355kg) motorcycle was not one of them.

But for Harley-Davidson's hard core of traditionalist buyers it could do no wrong. They may have baulked at the new-fangled telescopic forks, then the rear suspension, then the electric start, but they went on buying the bikes year on year. These American touring riders would keep on trading in for yet another big Harley, simply because there was nothing else that gave the same riding experience.

But what was good for the traditionalist was not necessarily good for the company. While FL sales remained constant, the market was expanding all around it, part of the reason why Harley-Davidson had only 6 per cent of the American motorcycle market in 1965. That

of the V-twin nicknames were) kept the hydraulic tappets and alloy heads, but used a Sportster-style top end. The result was a useful power boost to 60bhp, which by 1968 had climbed again, to 65bhp at 5,400rpm, this time thanks to a Tillotson diaphragm carburettor and improved porting. Perhaps of more relevance to most riders was its solid wall of torque in the mid-range –

showed just how far out on a limb it was. The big twins sold well to American riders, but had little relevance to anyone else – only 3 per cent of Harleys were exported in the mid-sixties. They were bigger, heavier and far more expensive than anything else, and public taste was moving on. None of this would have mattered too much if Harley-Davidson had been making good profits. Its turnover nearly doubled between 1958 and 1965, but profits remained low. The generous racing budget, the purchase and running of half Aermacchi, plus the fact that home-grown Harleys were expensive to make, all led to one conclusion – Milwaukee was running out of money.

So in 1965 the family firm went public for the first time. It was careful to maintain control – various Harleys and Davidsons still held more than half the stock and made up seven of the nine-strong Board. The flotation certainly brought in extra money, and Harley-Davidson proceeded to spend it on new capital equipment and a big advertising campaign. Sales did

increase the following year, to over 36,000, but fell the year after and the year after that. Within a couple of years of the flotation, Harley-Davidson was back to square one: it had run out of money and was forced to think again.

Selling the business lock, stock and barrel appeared to be the only answer. As it happened, there were two takers, keen to buy up Harley-Davidson. Bangor Punta was one, a massive firm with assets of $267 million and fingers in all sorts of pies. Bangor Punta was keen, but had a reputation as an asset stripper. The American Machine and Foundry Company (AMF) was even bigger and had a strong engineering background. The Harley management favoured AMF which had promised to allow it to keep control. Better still, Chairman Rodney C. Gott was a Harley enthusiast! After a fight (Bangor Punta was threatening legal action at one point), the shareholders accepted the deal, and Harley-Davidson formally became a subsidiary of AMF in January 1969. It was a family firm no longer, and never would be again.

OPPOSITE, ABOVE
Another rare bike: 1965 was the only year of the Electra Glide Panhead. The Shovelhead appeared the year after.

OPPOSITE, BELOW
Inside the early Aermacchi singles were race bikes trying to get out, which did Harley-Davidson no harm at all.

BELOW
Full dresser equipment is provided for this Electra – panniers, monstrous seat, screen and spotlights – all have become part of the Electra Glide look.

Specifications

1962 Harley-Davidson 250 Sprint
Engine

Type	Air-cooled 4-stroke single, ohv
Capacity	15ci (246cc)
Bore x stroke	65 x 71mm
Compression ratio	8.5:1
Carburation	1-inch Dell 'Orto
Power	18bhp @ 7,500rpm

Transmission

Clutch	Wet, multiplate
Gearbox	Four-speed
Final drive	Chain

Chassis

Frame	Steel spine type
Front suspension	Telescopic fork
Rear suspension	Swinging arm, twin dampers
Front brake	Cable-operated drum
Rear brake	Rod-operated drum
Front tyre	3.00-17
Rear tyre	3.00-17
Wheelbase	52in (132cm)
Seat height	29in (74cm)
Fuel capacity	4 gallons (US)
Kerb weight	270lb (122kg)

Specifications

1967 Harley-Davidson Electra Glide
Engine

Type	Air-cooled V-twin, ohv
Capacity	74ci (1207cc)
Bore x stroke	87.3 x 100.8mm
Compression ratio	8:1
Carburation	1.5-inch Tillotson
Power	65 bhp @ 5,400rpm

Transmission

Clutch	Dry, multi-plae
Gearbox	Four-speed
Final drive	Chain

Chassis

Frame	Tubular steel
Front suspension	Telescopic fork
Rear suspension	Swinging arm, twin dampers
Front brake	8in (20cm) drum
Rear brake	8in drum
Front tyre	5.00-16
Rear tyre	5.00-16
Wheelbase	60in (152cm)
Seat height	31.3in (80cm)
Fuel capacity	5 gallons (US)
Kerb weight	783lb (355kg)

Chapter Eight
The 1970s:
Uppers and Downers

**The Super Glide as milestone – Development of the Sportster – The two-stroke traillies –
The AMF story – The XLCR – Low Rider – Loss of police business – AMF says no**

Something had to change ...

Where Harley-Davidson was concerned, 1970 could be remembered for any number of things – perhaps the 100cc Baja off-roader? Maybe not. Or maybe regaining the world motorcycle speed record (who remembers that)? Or the first full year of AMF ownership? – some would rather forget that altogether. No: what made 1970 special was another milestone bike – the Super Glide.

Technically, there was very little new about the Super Glide (or FX). It was no bigger or faster or more advanced than any other Harley (let alone any other motorcycle). But it was as much a milestone as the Knucklehead and Sportster. For the first time, it mixed and matched existing parts, threw in some restyling and came up with something that looked quite different. It was cost-effective, in fact, effective overall, and this principle has formed the basis of Harley-Davidson's success ever since.

Perhaps if funds hadn't been so tight for Harley-Davidson at the time, the Super Glide would never have happened, but in 1970 it needed something new to sell, and quickly. AMF was about to make its big push on production, the motorcycle market still boomed, and Harley-Davidson didn't have the time or money to develop a genuinely new bike. The Super Glide was the best solution, and the person to thank for it was William G. Davidson.

Known to all and sundry as Willie G., this third generation Davidson had joined the family firm in 1963 after working as a designer for Ford and Brooks Stevens. He was a professional who happened to have grown up with motorcycles but had plenty of design experience outside the

industry. So he was ideally placed to interpret what motorcycle riders (or to be more accurate, Harley riders) wanted, and to put it into practice.

The Super Glide was a perfect example of this. For years, Milwaukee was a little disdainful as far as the custom movement was concerned. It may have consisted of a sizable slice of Harley-Davidson riders, but it also had associations with the outlaw element. On the other hand, customizers' money was as good as anyone else's, and numerous dealers were making a good living from selling custom parts or building up complete bikes. The Super Glide was the first official acceptance that this was a legitimate way to treat a Harley – not that it was very radical by custom standards. This was the time when front forks were growing longer with each succeeding year, high-rise handlebars sprouted ever upwards, and tombstone seats reached for the sky. The Super Glide owed more to the earlier California Bobber customs being a long, low machine with lowish bars and a lightweight front end. But, by Harley-Davidson's standards, it was radical indeed – so much so that it published pictures of this 'concept bike' and carefully judged reaction to it before going ahead. That innate caution, so much a part of the company since the beginning, still remained.

A glance at the parts list would have revealed how little was new about the Super Glide. It used the frame, engine and gearbox straight out of the 1200cc touring FL, coupled to the lighter-weight forks, 19-inch front wheel and small headlamp from the XLCH (hence 'FX'). To save weight, the FL's electric start and big battery were ditched and the tank was a new, smaller version of the big bike's (later swapped for the slimmer 3.5-gallon from the Sprint). In

fact, the only genuinely new part was the glassfibre 'boatail' rear end. Harley-Davidson had in-house knowledge on the subject of glassfibre since buying up the Tomahawk company in the sixties (a range of golf cars was the result) – another example of Willie G. making good use of what was already available. It did away with the need for a heavyweight rear mudguard and contributed much to the look of the bike. It was, in the author's opinion (and there's nothing like a bit of controversy), clearly inspired by the Norton Commando Fastback, which had gone on sale the year before. Whoever thought of it first, the styling department was so enthusiastic that it made the boatail an option on the Sportster that year.

Ironically, it was this one new part that proved the biggest block to Super Glide sales. It was just a little too radical for most Harley riders, and most FX buyers replaced the boatail with a standard mudguard. One dealer later revealed that he only sold two FXs with the glassfibre rear-end in place. Of course, the classic bike world, being what it is, now reveres the reviled boatail as a classic of its time; but this could easily be because so many of them were

lost or thrown away by owners still entrenched in their conservative ways.

Whatever you think of the Super Glide's style, it actually had some practical benefits. It offered the FL's power and torque, but weighed 125lb (57kg) less, so it could manage 108mph (174km/h) where the big twin couldn't crack the ton; it was a full second faster on the standing quarter and averaged 47mpg (17km per litre) when tested by *Cycle World*. Of course, it wouldn't handle as well as the Sportster, but it did open up a whole new market – there were riders for whom the FL had grown too fat, while the Sportster was thought by some to be lacking in muscle. The holy trinity of Harley riders – tourists, sportsters and customizers – was finally complete.

Not that it was an immediate hit: sales got off to a slow start (it was outsold by both Sportster and big twin) but improved when the boatail was dropped, and improved again when an electric start FXE appeared. But the Super Glide's real success lay in what Harley-Davidson could achieve simply by swapping around a few parts. It was a lesson well learned.

Meanwhile, the Sportster wasn't having

It is hard to believe now that Harley-Davidson sold two-stroke trail bikes, but it did. They were the last chapter in the Aermacchi story in which Harley tried to compete head-on with the Japanese. It was perhaps the best way to learn that it could not.

things all its own way. It was selling better than ever. Thanks to AMF's production boost, sales tripled in the early seventies from around 8,500 in 1970 to over 10,000 in 1971, then 18,000, then 20,000 and so on. One out of three Harleys sold was a Sportster, and the company couldn't have survived without it. On the other hand, it had

been overtaken in the horsepower race: the Honda CB750, Kawasaki's Z900 and ultra-fast two-strokes, all were leaving the Sportster behind.

The old 54ci/883cc (circa 1957, with origins extending further back) had reached its limit in tuning terms, and the only answer was to

RIGHT, BELOW
In the seventies, the Electra Glide faced a new challenge from Japan – the Goldwing. But the big Honda was only partly successful in breaking into Harley-Davidson's traditional market, and Harley managed to survive.

OPPOSITE, ABOVE
A 1970 Sportster, now well established as part of the Harley-Davidson line-up. But it still used cable-operated drum brakes to stop a 500-lb motorcycle.

OPPOSITE, BELOW
By this time, the Sportster was no longer one of the fastest things on the road and Harley-Davidson opted to enlarge the engine and detune it, keeping the detuning relatively mild. In any case, it still went on selling like hot cakes.

make it bigger. So it was bored out to 997cc – in other words, the classic 61ci (1000cc) capacity was back! Little else changed (though the Tillotson carburettor was replaced by a Bendix/Zenith) and power was increased modestly from 56bhp to 61bhp, now at 6,200rpm. According to *Cycle World*'s figures, the latest XLCH of 1972 was 4mph (6km/h) faster than the last 883 it tested (116mph/187km/h) and used less fuel (43mpg/15km per litre). Strangely, despite the greater torque, almost identical weight, and low first gear, it was left behind by the old bike until past 60mph (97km/h), when it pulled decisively ahead. None of which was enough to meet the opposition: but rather than try and supertune the Sportster in a vain attempt to keep up, Harley-Davidson sensibly kept the tuning relatively mild, and it went on selling like hot cakes, even if it wasn't the fastest thing on the road. In any case, if this was of concern to macho riders, they could console themselves with the fact that the Sportster still needed a good manly kick start to wake it up – electric starts were still for the plain XLH, and for tourists. Less welcome was the old cable-operated drum front brake, which just wasn't up to the demands

Although its image was built on that of the slim XLCH, many early sportsters were sold in this XL form, with large, fat fuel tanks plus optional panniers and screen to turn them into mini full-dress tourers.

of a 116mph 500lb (227kg) motorcycle. At long last the solution came in 1973, with a proper hydraulic disc.

Another thing that required a revamp in the early seventies were Harley-Davidson's small bikes. The company had persevered with Aermacchi products, only to see them overtaken yet again by the Japanese, although it is true that the Sprint had had a few updates – notably the 350cc version, the trail bike SX and in 1973, electric start. None of this was enough, and the range was dropped the following year. Two-strokes seemed to be the future, and a suitable base was the Rapido, a 125cc commuter bike that had appeared in 1968. It sold steadily enough, but was hardly the thing to break into the burgeoning trail-bike market. The Baja 100 was Harley's first response, a pure off-road scrambler that used a sleeved-down version of the 125. It was a peaky, high-seated machine with high ground clearance, expensive for its time, and was dropped after three years.

Selling to a wider market was the TX125. This had all the right attributes for taking on the Japanese trailsters – off-road looks and knobbly tyres but with full road equipment, and the 125 single was updated with oil injection. Interestingly, it came with an alternative sprocket for extra low off-road gearing, which for many riders was perhaps a needless complication. It certainly looked right, and at the time was rated as economical, fine for the easier trails, but a little lacking in performance.

The answer came in the form of a 175 version, which appeared the year after, and the SX250 in 1975. But it was a measure of just how fast the competition was advancing that what was considered acceptable in the early seventies began to appear slightly unfinished a few years later. Reading the spec sheet of the 250, it must have appeared well up to scratch: 250cc oil injection two-stroke with CDI ignition, five-speed gearbox, Marzocchi suspension (five-way adjustable on the back), even an extra hole tapped into the head for a second plug. But *Cycle World* wasn't impressed when it tested an SX250 in early 1975. First, the gearbox blew up, then its replacement did the same, and it was considered overgeared for off-road use. It described the bike's appearance as 'rustic' and there were numerous details that made it unsuitable for off-road use. And, as ever, it struggled to compete

with the Japanese on price. On the other hand, Harley-Davidson sold 11,000 of them in that first year. It may have been its best-selling bike in 1975, but sales plummeted the following year. Wisely, perhaps, Harley killed off all its little bikes in 1978 and has never sold one to the public since.

Takeovers are never easy and Harley-Davidson and AMF appeared to be lacking in synergy. Though both were engineering-based, one was a long-established family firm which had made much the same type of product all its life, while the other had fingers in numerous pies with professional careerist managers in charge.

Naturally, there was some suspicion among Milwaukee diehards when the new broom began to sweep. Although there were assurances that much would stay the same (certainly the Board remained dominated by Davidsons and Harleys) this was, to use a technical term, hogwash.

AMF's Chairman Rodney C. Gott had a clear idea of what had to be done with Harley-Davidson. The motorcycle market was expanding, Harley-Davidson could sell more bikes. So, why not boost production as rapidly as possible, increase sales and thus generate the funds needed to produce new models? It was the right strategy, but implemented in such a hurry

that quality flew out of the window.

AMF certainly did what it said it would do – Harley-Davidson built/imported just over 27,000 motorcycles in 1969; well over 37,000 in 1971 and nearly 60,000 in the following year. In other words, the output of the old Juneau Avenue plant had been more than doubled in three years. It was quite an achievement, but something had to give, and that was the reason why AMF Harleys got such a bad name. Rodney Gott later admitted that the company had got it wrong and was quoted in Peter Reid's *Well Made in America* as saying: 'I'm afraid we concentrated too much on expanding production and not enough on quality. Our only concern was to get the motorcycles out as fast as we could. We felt that if we took time out to redesign the product at that point we could have kissed goodbye to the motorcycle boom.'

However, he added that part of the problem was the Milwaukee management and its resistance to change. On the other hand, some long-serving Harley-Davidson employees are of the opinion that if AMF had consulted them, rather than steam-rollering the changes in, then maybe it all would have worked out better.

Whatever, plans were already in place to expand production still further. AMF had a large under-utilized plant at York, Pennsylvania, and set about moving all motorcycle assembly there; engine- and gearbox-building remained at Juneau Avenue. There was huge disruption and possible inco-ordination between the two plants and many Milwaukee workers were laid off, causing industrial relations to suffer. The result was similar to the Aermacchi problem though less extreme – two plants, 700 miles apart.

The first York Harley rolled off the line in

February 1973, but even then it was clear that the plan wasn't going well. So Ray Tritten, who was a sort of AMF company doctor, was brought in and didn't like what he found: Harley-Davidson was losing money on every bike it sold; there seemed to be a thorough-going lack of professionalism in the engineering, marketing and spare parts departments; top management was still complacent about Japanese competition; dealers had subsidized financial packages that cost Harley-Davidson a lot of money; and finally, AMF itself was cordially disliked.

With characteristic energy, Tritten got on with the job, reducing costs, cutting out bottlenecks, initiating proper forecasting. Perhaps one of the more significant changes was the arrival of Jeff Bleustein to the engineering department. A former associate professor of engineering at Yale, Bleustein brought in more trained engineers to work on Harley's new model programme. One thing that came to light was that the company had spent $10 million on developing an 1100cc version of the Shovelhead. Precious money and time, in other words, on an

The XR750 was Harley-Davidson's long-awaited replacement for the side-valve KR. Based on a sleeved-down Sportster 883, it was tailor-made for American race tracks, and went on to dominate the dirt tracks.

engine decades old which had become a byword for oil leaks, vibration and unreliability. Changes had to be made.

Change they did when Tritten put an AMF man called Vaughn Beals directly in control at Milwaukee. One of the first things Beals did, as newly incumbent executives often do, was to take the top layer of management away for a week. The result of that meeting in Pinehurst, North Carolina was that at long last Harley-Davidson had a long-term engineering strategy. In the short term, the existing V-twin would be gradually improved, and this was the engine that became the Evolution. For the future, and this was the radical part, AMF would fund a whole new family of engines – 500 to 1300cc and with two to six cylinders.

This was the NOVA programme, which Beals and Co. considered to be the only way to ensure Harley-Davidson's long-term survival, designed to meet the Japanese head-on. To save costs, the new family would share many components; to save time (even Bleustein's upgraded department couldn't cope with a project

LEFT
It is odd that Willie G. and the stylists failed to capitalize on the XR's success with an XR-styled sportster.

BELOW
The original iron-barrelled XR twin was not a success, but aluminium barrels allowed higher compression and, eventually, over 90bhp.

this big), the design contract went to Porsche.

At the time, it all looked quite feasible. AMF had faith in the Beal/Bleustein strategy of product-led recovery and, for a while, money wasn't a problem. 'Anything I asked for in engineering we got,' Bleustein later recalled. In all, AMF spent $10 million on NOVA. If everything had gone to plan, six-cylinder Harleys might well have been on the market by the mid-eighties.

But even with NOVA and Evolution going full steam ahead, Harley-Davidson still needed to survive in the meantime. It was time for Willie G. to come up with something new, and he did. In fact, there were two things: what was interesting was that one was a dead-end – the other confirmed what had already been observed from experience of the Super Glide. To sell, a Harley had to look the way a Harley always had and (this is a safe suggestion) always will. First

fairing to the all-black colour scheme, it looked like no other factory Harley before or since. It personified mean, moody performance, though of course this still wasn't a café racer in the European sense. The classic café racers of the fifties and sixties, such as BSAs or Nortons, were far closer to the concept – low-set bars and rear-set footrests, and lots of polished alloy. The XLCR was an essentially American interpretation.

But though it looked like no other Harley which had gone before, it was not necessary to scratch very hard to find some familiar parts beneath the surface. The rear subframe and some of the suspension was from the XR750 racer, while the front of the frame was pure Sportster. The engine was Sportster 1000, though painted black (to match the black frame, tank, seat, wheels – well, you get the idea!). In other words, it was a continuation of the FX philosophy – take what you've already got and rearrange it to create something else. It looked faster than the Sportster but in practice was not, and with virtually the same weight and power, contemporary road tests actually placed it a few miles per hour slower on top speed. With its long wheelbase, the CR was no nimble sports bike either (and it still weighed over 500lb/227kg) but it was perhaps intended to be a bike you really did just ride to the café on a Sunday morning rather than a serious sportster. Whatever, the XLCR was a sales flop. In its best year (1977) 1,923 were sold; for each one, Harley sold six standard Sportsters. Even fewer found buyers the following year, and the XLCR died a natural death.

But if the CR was a dead-end, the Low Rider, which appeared later that year, was a real pointer to the future. It took the basic Super Glide (which remained part of the range right through the seventies) and added several pure chopper touches. As a custom bike, the original Super Glide was pretty mild stuff, but as Willie G. said of the Low Rider at the time: 'we took the custom bubble and pushed it further'. So the forks were lengthened and raked. The rear dampers were shortened and a king and queen seat added to give that low-riding 27-inch saddle and buckhorn bars were discarded in favour of short, flat, straight ones.

The result was not a flashy, look-at-me chopper, but something more contained, more subtle. It was a blend of old and new, rather than

An Electra Glide Shovelhead with comparatively few add-ons. The accessories business was to become (so it seemed) as big as the motorcycle industry itself.

of the two was the XLCR, which went on sale in 1977. 'CR' stood for Café Racer, which to most people indicates how much of a departure this was for Harley-Davidson.

The story goes that Willie G. designed it, with himself in mind, as the bike he would like to own. The prototype was shown to the public, who were suitably enthusiastic, so into production it went. From its alloy wheels, through to its twin-disc front-end and bikini

RIGHT
By the mid-seventies, Harley-
Davidson realized that the
Electra Glide sold because of
the way it looked, rather than in
spite it. A true attempt at
modernization came with the
1980 FLT.

OPPOSITE, ABOVE
The Super Glide FX was a
milestone bike, the first to be
offered by Harley (or indeed
anybody else) aimed at
customizers.

OPPOSITE, BELOW
Squint a little, ignore the
Shovelhead rocker boxes, and
this could be a big twin from the
sixties (or indeed, the eighties,
fifties, nineties ...)

simply a nostalgic indulgence. The instruments mounted on the Fat Bob tank, and the 1903-style tank script were obvious references to older Harley-Davidsons, but the alloy wheels and twin-disc front-end were bang up-to-the-minute. The FXS Low Rider simply looked good. And buyers responded to it in droves. It was only available for a few months in 1977, but over 3,700 were sold. Over the next few years it outsold every other Harley, apart from the basic Sportster. The Super Glide may have been the start of the Harley factory custom niche market, but the FXS made it a major consideration.

Harley-Davidson learned a very important lesson, not to mention every other manufacturer – that style, if potent enough, can override

performance. The Low Rider's stiff, harsh ride was uncomfortable; its long raked forks did little to absorb small bumps, and the short bars which looked so good made the steering very heavy at low speeds. But nobody who bought a Low Rider seemed to mind – they were buying a look and a dream as much as a motorcycle, and that too was a pointer to the way things were going. It is worth emphasizing the point. The Low Rider looked like a fresh model, but very little was actually new. Jeff Bleustein is quoted as saying: 'In the five year interim before we could bring the Evolution engine on stream, he [Willie G.] performed miracles with decals and paint. A line here and there and we'd have a new model. It's what enabled us to survive during those years.'

But while the public may have been flocking to buy Low Riders, the U.S. police, who for so long had been loyal customers, were looking elsewhere. Kawasaki got its timing right when it began to tout police business in 1975, just as Harley-Davidson's problems of quality were reaching a crescendo. Not surprisingly, with modern, reliable, and often cheaper motorcycles, it began to gain police contracts at Harley's expense. Some forces were so disgruntled with the twin's unreliability that they actually stopped testing the bikes and it was to be a decade before Harley-Davidson began to claw its way back into the police force market.

Competition for these prestigous contracts were reminiscent of the old pre-war battles with

Indian, but there was to be another historic repetition in the seventies. The long sales boom in motorcycles was starting to level off, and in 1978, Harley-Davidson began to demand that tariffs be imposed on imported bikes, which it said were being dumped on the U.S. market at unfair discounts. This is a repeat of what had occurred in 1950, but with British imports. At that time, Harley's case was ruined when restrictive practices against its own dealers came under the spotlight. And 28 years on, exactly the same thing happened. This time, dealers claimed that the Aermacchi bikes were simply outdated compared with the opposition. The Government responded that if that was the case it only had itself to blame, and threw out the request. Harley would have to go on selling against discounted Hondas for a few years yet.

The year 1979 saw Harley's best sales ever. The 80ci capacity (not seen since the side-valve days) returned as a 1340cc option on the tourers, Super Glides and Low Riders. Work was proceeding apace on the Evolution and Willie G.'s ever-inventive styling department was, in the meantime, producing new bikes from the same old parts. But as far as AMF was concerned, time was running out. Harley-Davidson was making profits, but very small ones, and nothing like enough to fund the NOVA programme. According to a team of consultants, NOVA needed about $70 million to reach production. There was a time when AMF would have signed the cheque, but Rodney Gott had chosen an accountant named Tom York as his successor. York was no motorcyclist, and saw greater profit potential in the industrial side of AMF's business. Over 10 years, AMF had put a great deal of money into Harley-Davidson, so far with very little return. It was time for a change of ownership.

OPPOSITE, ABOVE
The XLCR. 'CR' stands for 'Café Racer', though rather more in the American sense than the European. Too European for the Yanks, too American for the Limeys, perhaps?

OPPOSITE, BELOW
By the end of the decade, Harley-Davidson had proved itself well able to cash in on the Electra Glide cult, the ultimate for many being this Classic, fully dressed with luggage, fairing, spotlights, etc.

Specifications

1979 Sportster XLS1000

Engine

Type	Air-cooled, 4-stroke V-twin
Capacity	61ci (997cc)
Bore x stroke	81 x 97mm
Compression ratio	9.0:1
Carburation	38mm Keihin

Transmission

Clutch	Wet, multiplate
Gearbox	4-speed
Final drive	Chain

Chassis

Frame	Tubular steel
Front suspension	Telescopic fork, 6.9in (18cm) travel
Rear suspension	Swinging arm, twin dampers, 3.75in (10cm) travel
Front brake	Twin discs, 10in (25cm)
Rear brake	Single disc, 11.5in (29cm)
Front tyre	MJ90-19
Rear tyre	MT90-19
Wheelbase	59.6in (151cm)
Seat height	31.5in (80cm)
Fuel capacity	2.25 gallons (U.S.)
Weight	541lb (245kg)

Specifications

1978 Electra Glide FLH80

Engine

Type	Air-cooled, 4-stroke V-twin
Capacity	82ci (1338cc)
Bore x stroke	89 x 108mm
Compression ratio	8.0:1
Carburation	38mm Keihin

Transmission

Clutch	Wet, multiplate
Gearbox	4-speed
Final drive	Chain

Chassis

Frame	Tubular steel
Front suspension	Telescopic fork
Rear suspension	Swinging arm, twin dampers
Front brake	Single disc, 9.7in (25cm)
Rear brake	Single disc, 9.7in
Front tyre	5.10-16
Rear tyre	5.10-16
Wheelbase	61.5in (156cm)
Seat height	29.9–31.4in (76–80cm)
Fuel capacity	5.0 gallons (U.S.)
Weight	752lb (341kg)

Chapter Nine
The 1980s:
Back from the Brink

**The Tour Glide – The Sturgis brings belt-drive – Buy-Back – Japanese methods – Tariffs at last –
The Evolution – The Softail – The Sportster 883/1200 – XR1000 – Buell steps in – The Springer –
The FXRS & Convertible – Thank you, Mr. President**

The closest the company had ever come to complete closure.

In 1973 Harley-Davidson commanded over three-quarters of the U.S. big bike market. By 1980, that had shrunk to less than a third. But as AMF celebrated its tenth year of Harley-Davidson ownership (actually, it's unlikely that it 'celebrated' anything of the sort) there was finally something to be cheerful about. The reinvigorated engineering department under Jeff Bleustein was at last starting to come up with the goods in the form of the redesigned FLT and belt-driven Sturgis. Evolution was still a few years away but it finally looked as if Harley-Davidson was taking model development seriously.

In fact, the Tour Glide was as near as it could get to being an all-new bike while retaining the old Shovelhead engine. First and foremost, the old engine was rubber-mounted, which doesn't sound all that radical but made a huge difference in practice. There were rubber block mounts at the front and the swing-arm pivots, plus adjustable locating links at the front and the top. It worked a treat, allowing vibration through when idling but virtually eliminating it once the bike was on the move. This anti-vibration set-up was underestimated at the time but has since been applied to nearly every Harley model and played a huge part in making them acceptable to non-Harley riders.

The frame was new too, consisting of a substantial steel backbone, two downtubes and new swinging arm. The real step forward, though, was at the front: by mounting the forks offset to the steering head, Harley was able to combine a steepish steering-head angle (for quicker steering) and a long 5.88in (15cm) of trail (for stability).

For the first time, a big Harley had light steering and handling while retaining its stability. There were other signs that the frame's designers were determined to address traditional Harley-Davidson weaknesses: it had a decent 35 degrees of steering lock, and there were two extra inches of ground clearance so that you could lean through the corners without fear of grounding out earlier than any other bike on the road.

The engine itself was given some changes to mark time until the Evolution came on stream – notably electronic ignition, a new exhaust system (both quieter and more powerful, according to the press release), and a spin-off oil filter. Perhaps more significant was the new fifth gear, the first time seen on a Harley twin though, as ever, the gearbox remained separate from the engine. Primary drive was still by duplex chain, but the final-drive chain acquired complete enclosure and an oil bath; Harley-Davidson claimed it would last up to 20,000 miles (32,186km) as a result. It was a real step forward and certainly cheaper than a shaft, though it was odd that Harley developed and paid for this enclosure so soon before the Sturgis' belt-drive appeared.

As for the rest of the bike, new twin headlamp fairing, new twin-disc front end, new five-gallon tank – even new instruments – all proclaimed that Milwaukee (plus now York, of course) were serious about model development. The magazines appreciated this, and praised the FLT in appropriate terms when it went on sale at a little over $6,000. It actually topped a group test conducted by *Cycle World* against a Goldwing, BMW and the three other Japanese heavyweights of the time, something the FLH would never have been able to do.

Later that year came the Sturgis. Belt-driven Harleys were nothing new – the founders took nearly ten years to fit a chain, and belt-drive kits had been on offer for a while. But the Sturgis was the first production motorcycle to be offered with toothed belts for both primary and final drives. Kawasaki was first with a belt final, but that was restricted to one model. By contrast, the Harley-Davidson system was so successful that it was eventually extended to every bike in the range, though the primary later went back to a conventional chain. Although the belts cost more than chains, their advantages were many: the primary belt required no lubrication or tensioner as the belts did not stretch in the same way that a chain did; no primary chain oil meant no leaks and a drier, longer-lived clutch. As for the 1.5-inch (4-cm) wide final belt, there was no more messing with lube can and spanners, while it had a life of 20,000 miles (32,000km) without (as some saw it) the aesthetic downside of a full chaincase. The belt was quieter than a chain (a

real plus point for Harley) and smoothed out the drive. Fears that belts would snap under the Harley's considerable torque proved groundless; as someone at the time pointed out, cars with far more torque had used toothed-belt cam-drives without trouble for years.

The only puzzle was that Harley chose to introduce its belt, not on the long-distance FL, but on the Low Rider. The FXB-80 Sturgis was no more than a standard Low Rider with belts instead of chains. Unlike the new FLT, it stayed with the old four-speed gearbox (though with a higher second) and solid-mounted engine. Neither did it use the FLT's clever geometry, sticking to a more traditional 31 degrees of fork rake, and it ground out on corners the way big Harleys traditionally did (and the FLT did not). And despite the new triple discs, the brakes were heavy and ineffective (brakes remain a Harley-Davidson weakness to this day), the narrow bars made the Sturgis heavy to steer, and it was slow off the mark. But it looked good in its all-black

A twin-headlight Tour Glide (FLT) overtakes some more traditional Harleys. With its rubber-mounted engine, 5-speed gearbox, electronic ignition, new frame and ancillaries, the FLT was a concerted effort by Harley-Davidson to produce a modern tourer around the Shovelhead.

An XR1000, though this is a mildly customized version. The street-racer XR seemed to run counter to the prevailing Harley philosophy of mixing and matching existing parts. Exclusive and expensive it may have been, but it did inspire the first Buell.

livery with red highlights, and you couldn't deny that the belt drive was a real step forward.

While the Bleustein-inspired engineering department was coming up with some belated goods, Harley-Davidson itself was in deep trouble. Over the next few years it was to come closer to collapse than ever before. After ten years in charge, AMF had had enough: it had spent a great deal of money on new plant, reorganization, equipment of the York factory and getting Evolution, NOVA and other updates up and running. At the end of all this, Harley-Davidson was making only very small profits and market share was diminishing by the month. It only needed Tom York's new emphasis on AMF's other interests to drastically alter the situation. Suddenly, long-term investment became more difficult to get. The NOVA programme faltered, and was shelved.

But Vaughn Beals had been associated with Harley long enough to know that the company

had potential, so he recommended what became known as Buy-Back, and he did it in a very subtle manner. In late 1980 he issued an internal paper which recommended that AMF sell Harley-Davidson outright. And when AMF management agreed to the idea, it turned out that Beals had already set up a management buy-out scheme ready and waiting.

Negotiations dragged on through the spring of 1981, not only among AMF's top ranks, but with Citicorp bankers who were interested in financing the buy-out. There were all sorts of complications (not least when the *Wall Street Journal* ran an unfounded story that Honda was interested in buying), but finance was eventually obtained and a price of $80 million agreed. Well, not quite agreed. Late one night, with pens poised to sign the agreement, neither side would give way on a half-million dollar difference on the price. Vaughn Beals suggested they toss a coin for it, which they did, and he lost.

But nobody minded, and the news that Harley-Davidson was independent ('the eagle soars alone') once more was greeted with general euphoria by workforce, dealers and riders. On 16 June, the management rode out of York on a celebratory independence trip to Milwaukee. Dealers' premises were visited, where AMF signs were jubilantly unscrewed or painted over. The press loved it, and so did everyone associated with the company.

It was tempting, in the general atmosphere, to cast AMF in the light of big, bad corporation and that now it was free from its clutches and heavy-handed management, Harley-Davidson would prosper once more. But in point of fact, AMF actually did the company a great deal of good: it saved it from Bangor Punta, made long-term investments and left Harley-Davidson a good deal more modern and flexible than it had been in the old days. Turnover rocketed from $49 million in 1969 to $300 million by 1980. Without all that investment it is doubtful that Harley would have made it through the seventies at all.

But while the eagle may have been soaring alone, it no longer had AMF's hot air currents to keep it afloat. The early eighties were tough times for makers of motorcycles all over the world, and for Harley more than most. The market took a nose-dive, and the Japanese responded by discounting bikes that were already cheaper than the Milwaukee twins. Harley's market share consequently slid further downhill and in 1981 it actually lost its lead of the big bike market for the first time in decades. While Beals and Co. were on their victory ride, 6,000 Harleys were sitting in dealers' showrooms, unsold.

It was not only the market that was against Harley-Davidson's recovery. The company had no money, and it now owed $80 million to various institutions, the interest alone being a major drain on its resources. Quality was still a major problem as Japanese bikes kept on improving. It was said that half the bikes coming down the assembly line at York were missing parts. Dealers found themselves with the old familiar task of making good before a sale (let alone after) and Harleys still vibrated and leaked oil. The year or two immediately after buy-back, when Harley-Davidson lost a lot of money and was struggling to survive, was the low point. In two years, nearly half the workforce was made redundant.

Fortunately, the buy-out management was making a determined effort to turn the company round. And it did so by completely reorganizing the way it built bikes, adopting methods which the Japanese were already using to very good effect. There were three main strands:

Just-in-time inventory: instead of huge stocks of parts waiting to be used, getting rusty and obsolete, only those parts immediately needed were sent to the line. Costs fell, quality improved.

Employee involvement: the skills of the ones who knew most about the job (i.e. the people doing it) were enlisted to further help the drive towards quality. The shopfloor influenced decisions rather than having them imposed on them by remote management.

Finally, *Statistical Operator Control* gave every worker the statistical training to monitor their own quality and output. This all sounds deceptively simple – in reality, it is far more difficult for managers to obtain a consensus decision than impose one, but the results were undeniable. Money was saved – not just through more efficient production – but because the product was 'right first time', not needing to be expensively rectified in the factory, at the dealer's or, worst of all, under warranty.

While Harley-Davidson was finally getting to grips with its internal problems, it was about to receive a big boost in the outside world. Twice before, in 1951 and 1978, the company had sought tariff protection and in 1983 it finally got

While the development department busied itself with rubber mounts, belt-drive and Evolution, it was still possible to buy a traditional FLH in the early eighties.

it. What persuaded the ITC this time was the fact
that the Japanese bike makers had built up
massive stocks of unsold product in the United
States which, together with the discounting,
seemed to support Harley-Davidson's case that
they were using the country as a dumping
ground. So from April that year, a new tariff of
45 per cent was added to imports over 700cc. It
would fall to 35 per cent the following year, then
to 20, 15 then 10 per cent. Harley-Davidson had
its breathing space. Not that tariffs were the
complete answer. They had less effect than might
have been expected because some Japanese bikes
were downsized to 699cc to avoid the barrier,
while Honda and Kawasaki already had U.S.
plants which were soon making big bikes.
Nevertheless, 1983 and the tariff decision was a
turning point for Harley-Davidson. Losses
became profits, and even market share began to
recover. It had a mere 23.3 per cent of the big
bike (850cc+) market that year, but nearly 27 per
cent the year after. Neither was all of this due to
employee involvement and tariff reform – some
was down to the Evolution.

Fourteen years after the Evolution V-twin
first appeared, and nearly 20 after the design got
under way, it is easy to forget that it was intended
to be no more than a stopgap. When AMF
authorized the project in the mid to late
seventies, the Evolution was intended to fill the
breach until the all-new NOVA family came on
the scene. When the Evo was launched, a
selected group of dealers was shown a running
prototype of the V4 NOVA. They were evidently
told that the updated twin was good, but that this
was the real future for Harley-Davidson. But as
NOVA never happened, the stopgap has had to
serve ever since. Neither has this been out of
necessity: later in the eighties, when Harley-
Davidson finally had the resources to resurrect
NOVA, it chose to stick with Evolution.

As the name implied, the Evolution engine
was not all-new, merely a new top-end on the old
Knucklehead-based crankcase. And yet it was as
much a milestone as the Knucklehead had been
in 1936. The main difference was that, whereas
the thirties Harley leaped ahead of the
opposition, the Evo merely made a very efficent
job of catching up. First and foremost, it used
aluminium alloy cylinders (with cast iron liners)
in place of the Shovelhead's iron ones. Not only
were they lighter (the Evolution saved 20lb/9kg

over its predecessor) but they ran cooler. The
heads were all-new as well, with a much
narrower valve angle that allowed shorter,
straighter ports. The valves themselves were
smaller to increase air velocity, with milder
timing and more lift. Four long through-bolts
held both heads and barrels to the crankcase.

The valve train was lighter and the cam
lobes computer-designed, allowing the Evo to
safely realize 6,400rpm. The con-rods were
thicker (and ten times stronger, according to the
engineers) while the German Mahle pistons were
carefully designed to closer tolerances to allow
for expansion rates. Oil drain was improved too
(for long a Shovelhead problem), and a new two-
stage advance curve improved the electronic
ignition.

The Evolution, according to Harley, had

spent 5,600 hours on the dyno and run 750,000 miles (1207,000km) on the road. It did not leak oil, nor drink it; it produced 10 per cent more power than the Shovelhead and 15 per cent more torque – not that all-out performance was the aim. As Vaughn Beals observed at the Evolution's launch in late 1983: 'We know that quarter-mile and high speed isn't our game ... we want something a shade-tree mechanic can take care of.' In other words, Harley-Davidson had officially recognized that it couldn't compete in the horsepower race and sensibly pulled out. Still, the new bike proved usefully quicker than the old one – a second quicker over the quarter-mile in FLHTC guise, according to *Cycle World*.

It used no more fuel in the process, was good and torquey and best of all, reliable! For the first time in a long while, Milwaukee had come up with a substantially new engine that was as the product was trumpeted to be, Right First Time.

To begin with, only four Harleys benefited from the new engine, the FLTs and the touring/custom FXRT/S. But the company was careful to hedge its bets: alongside these rubber-mounted, five-speed bikes, it insisted on offering the old Shovelhead FLH and three FXs, complete with four-speed gearbox and solidly mounted engine.

The only other major change that year was the first Softail, the story being that Vaughn

Beals saw a hardtail-look Harley at a rally one year. It was built by Bill Davis, and cleverly hid its rear suspension units by mounting them horizontally, under the gearbox. It had a mere three inches of suspension travel, so for all practical purposes it was inferior to conventional bikes, but it looked like something out of the pre-Duo Glide fifties. Beals was impressed, bought the patent, and Softails have been part of Harley's line-up ever since. Again, it underlined the company's realization that the way a Harley-Davidson looked was at least as important as the way it rode – more so, for some.

All of this was good news, but behind the scenes things weren't going so well. Despite its

recovery, Harley-Davidson still owed millions to the banks who were on the verge of becoming difficult. The reason was simple: despite the improvement, it was still not making enough money to pay off loans. In 1985, Citicorp, one of the main lenders, announced that it intended to pull out, which was serious, as it logically meant the end of Harley-Davidson. Just days before the deadline, Richard Teerlink, Vaughn Beals and Tom Gelb managed to get replacement funds from Heller Financial. It was the closest the company had ever come to complete closure.

While all that was going on, some Harley dealers became so disgruntled with the new régime that they revolted and set up their own independent association. At the heart of the matter was a cut-back in margins, which dealers would get back if they invested in training and updated their marketing. Gradually, the rifts were healed and the independent Dealers Alliance shrank to a less threatening size and role. Surprisingly, much of the trouble was held to be caused by the way Vaughn Beals had put the new régime across. Jim Paterson, the motorcycle division president, was quoted in *Well Made in America* by Peter Reid as saying: 'You can't just tell someone who's been running a shop for 20 years that they don't know what the hell they're doing and then expect them to listen to what else you have to say.'

It was a measure of how successful the Evolution was (the official nickname of 'Blockhead' just never stuck) that a Sportster version appeared less than two years later. It followed all the same principles – alloy cylinders and heads, flat-top pistons and narrower valve angle – but was actually smaller, at 55ci (883cc), than the old one-litre Sportster twin. Not only was the 883cc an evocative number for Harley-watchers (the original Sportster had been that size right through the sixties) but it was just as fast as the old one-litre bike and cheaper to insure. There were actually over 200 new parts involved, and road tests confirmed that the 883 was indeed smoother and quieter than its predecessor. The first 883 also marked an attempt to reduce the cost of owning a Harley: at $3,995 on its home market, without five-speed box, rubber mounts or belt drive, it was a loss-leader. And if you traded it in for a bigger one, a refund was guaranteed on the new price. The idea was to tempt new riders into the Harley-Davidson fold. Not that this was a

A Softail Custom of 1987, and an accurate pointer to the way Harley-Davidson was going. The Softail frame, with rear shocks hidden behind the gearbox, gave the appearance of an authentic hardtail. Many buyers appreciated the Evo's ease of operation, but wanted the outlaw looks to go with it.

new idea. The pared-down XLX Sportster of 1982 was another loss-leader, and today's 883 seeks to do exactly the same thing.

None of which meant that the smallest Sportster was superior to the imported opposition. Three years after it first appeared, *Cycle World* compared an 883 with the Honda Shadow, Kawasaki Vulcan, Suzuki Intruder and Yamaha Virago, all of them ohc V-twins of 750–800cc. 'The 883 Sportster,' they concluded, 'unanimously brings up the rear. Harley's least

expensive motorcycle is slow, vibrates and is uncomfortable ... Harley builds some superb motorcycles, the Sportster 883 isn't one of them.'

Fortunately, for lovers of the Sportster, there was a happier alternative, even though it had long since been left behind in the performance race. The 67ci (1100cc) big brother appeared in 1985, with a bored-out version of the little 883 Evo to produce 12 per cent more power and 16 per cent more torque. They were not a startling improvement but enough to deliver a

13.5-second standing quarter, and a top speed of 104mph (167km/h). Otherwise, all was identical to the 883, with its four-speed gearbox, rigidly-mounted engine (no effete rubber buffers here) and chain-drive. It also relied on a single front-disc brake which the road testers noted needed a lot of effort to achieve any serious work. It was to become a familiar theme in Harley tests of the eighties and nineties when every other manufacturer's brakes improved year on year.

It wasn't long before the Sportster got

another capacity boost, to 74ci (1200cc) – another classic Milwaukee capacity. Bored out again, the V-twin's power and torque increased by small but useful percentages, enough to give the 1200 very quick in-gear acceleration (3.6 seconds 40–60mph/64–97km/h, according to *Cycle World*). That was partly down to under-gearing from the old four-speed box, which continued to hang on. Neither did rubber mounting make an appearance (criticism of vibration was becoming more marked these days): the Sportster was still chain- rather than belt-driven and the disc brake (a whole 0.3in/8mm bigger than before) was as hard work as ever.

Imperfect though it was, the Sportster 1200 remained Harley's sporting flagship (ten years on, it is still with us), but earlier in the eighties there had been an attempt to build something with more serious performance. The XR1000 was born when the newly-independent Harley-Davidson was facing its darkest hour. And yet in those first couple of years after the buy-back, the company spent much time and money developing a very limited production sports bike that sold in small numbers at a high price. When Harley was making a success of mixing and matching components to produce new models at low cost, the XR1000 went to the other extreme.

Although it used mostly Sportster frame and cycle parts, it had its own special cylinders and modified versions of the XR750's alloy heads. The complete engine was built in Milwaukee, but those special heads were sent all the way to Jerry Branch's tuning shop in California. Ports were polished, valve-springs carefully shimmed and titanium valve-collars installed. It was all expensive and labour-intensive and would never have been allowed in the AMF days. Not that the XR1000 twin was peaky and temperamental. It used the Sportster's relatively mild cams to give 70bhp at 5,600rpm and power from idling speed upwards. The factory promised 80bhp with different cams and pistons, and 100bhp from a race version. It was comfortably faster than any other Sportster (a 12.88-second quarter and 112-mph (180-km/h) top speed) though of course still a long way behind the Japanese litre-plus sports bikes. Unfortunately, the hand assembly and special parts didn't come cheaply, and the XR1000 cost over $6,000 when new – rather too much.

Interesting though it was, the XR1000 was

If the Softail Custom imitated a fifties California Bobber, then the Heritage Softail did the same in respect of the factory-fresh Hydra-Glide of the same era with its Japanese Showa forks hiding under the shrouds.

The ultimate retro? The Springer Softail went another step further (or backwards?) with an uprated version of Bill Harley's original Springer front fork. Whether this can be regarded as discarding 80 years of progress, or resisting obsolescence, depends on your own point of view.

something of a dead-end. On the other hand, its engine helped to spawn something far more significant – the Buell. Erik Buell worked as an engineer for Harley, and in his spare time raced a TZ750 Yamaha. He left to set up as a race-bike manufacturer, but his Buell RW750 was made immediately obsolete by a rule change. Then Harley-Davidson asked him to redesign the famous Lucifer's Hammer racer, while Vetter commissioned futuristic bodywork for a show bike. Combining the two with an XR1000 engine produced the Buell RR1000. Harley dealer Devin Battley was so impressed he (according to the story) smuggled Buell into a dealers' meeting where 20 colleagues said that they, too, wished to sell the RR1000. That in turn impressed Vaughn Beals, and Erik Buell got the batch of XR engines he needed to make the Buell a production reality. It was an odd mixture, with the rough-edged XR1000 twin rubber-mounted in a Buell frame with top-notch components from Marzocchi, Pirelli and Lockheed – all enclosed in that radical, all-enveloping bodywork. It still wasn't a straight-line match for the Japanese, but

certainly handled well; more importantly, the RR1000 inspired the birth of a new marque. Ten years later, Buell may have abandoned that original pure race-inspired sportster ideal, but it has become, in effect, the closest thing you can get to a Harley-Davidson sports bike.

With all these new models appearing, the Evolution twin so well received, and last-minute financing secured, few could deny that Harley-Davidson had at last turned the corner. Recovery might not have been complete, but it was at least well under way. It was at this point – in fact, only months after the Heller finance deal was signed – that the company took a step that was to secure its financial future: it went public. Selling shares isn't always the best thing a company can do. In theory, it has then to be run in the interests of shareholders rather than for a few people with an intimate knowledge of the product. Moreover, if confidence in a company is low, the new shares will sell for correspondingly low prices – control relinquished for very little return.

But by 1986 Harley-Davidson's recovery was a high-profile affair: everyone wanted to know how this American company, which a few years before had been at death's door, had turned itself around with Japanese business methods. Quality, market share and sales were all improving, and everyone seemed to know it. So when Harley-Davidson did offer shares in June 1986, the take-up was enthusiastic, and $90 million was raised. It was able to substantially reduce its borrowings and used a $50 million surplus to buy Holiday Rambler, a maker of motor homes. It is worth noting again that this money, which could have been used to resurrect the NOVA project, was instead spent on broadening the company's base. From a business viewpoint there was a lot to be said for this: it meant that Harley-Davidson no longer had all its eggs in one fluctuating motorcycle basket, and had the potential of retaining older customers who were beginning to think about hanging up their helmets and taking life easier. Spending all that money on NOVA was a high-risk venture by comparison and at the same time, with Evolution such a success, the management was coming to realize that Harley-Davidson's greatest asset was its association with big air-cooled V-twins. Anything else just wouldn't have been a Harley.

That realization was underlined by the Springer Softail which appeared in 1989. As front suspension it used no less than a slightly modified version of the original Springer front fork, the same one designed by Bill Harley about 80 years before. There were six springs rather than four, and a modern telescopic damper, but the leading link principle was the same. With stiffer and shorter travel (3.9in against 6.9in) than telescopic forks, the springers could bottom out on big bumps or under heavy braking. The narrow 21-inch (533-mm) front tyre that went with them didn't hold the road as well and no one could claim that the Springer was an advance in any direction, apart from looks. It was yet another example of form overriding function: the Springer's looks took precedence over performance. However, the Softail rear-end was given adjustable dampers (as a journalist pointed out at the time, there was only so much you could do with a mere 4in (10cm) of wheel travel).

In keeping with its retro looks, the Springer Softail retained the solidly-mounted engine (though it was an Evolution, the Shovelhead having finally died a death). This meant bad vibration at anything over 70mph (113km/h), and

60–65mph was a more natural and comfortable cruising speed. But then, the limited suspension was happier coping with such laid-back speeds and, if truth be told, so were the riders that bought Springer Softails.

If the Springer was the logical culmination of form over function, the Low Rider Sport (which actually made its debut a couple of years earlier, in 1987) was an attempt at something more sporting. To the basic Low Rider (which by this time had acquired the 82ci/1340cc rubber-mounted Evolution, five-speed gearbox and belt drive) was added better damped front forks, lower, flatter handlebars, a twin-disc front-end and longer-travel rear shocks. At the end of the day, no long wheelbase 570-lb (258-kg) twin was going to worry a Suzuki GSXR, but it certainly handled better than the standard FXR, and the longer travel rear shocks actually improved the ride. The only real complaint was that the low-barred riding positon was too sporty for long-haul cruising.

Harley-Davidson must have taken note of that, for in 1989 it came up with the Convertible. It had the Sport's suspension improvements, but added a quick-release screen and soft panniers. The idea was that you could tour on the bike long-distance, but for shorter trips remove the touring paraphernalia in a few minutes to produce a pared-down cruiser. Of course there were some compromises involved; the panniers weren't big enough to hold a full-face helmet, and the screen would never offer the same protection as a full fairing. Meanwhile, the Low Rider Sport did not possess the ultimate cruising looks of a Softail. But that didn't matter, as the Convertible was one of those rare compromises that actually came close to being the best of two worlds. Everyone agreed that the practical FXRS was a good basis for such a real-world bike, and it was. It also cost nearly $9,500 in the United States, or the same price as luxury cruisers. Harley could afford to charge prices like these because enough of the riding public was prepared to pay them.

It was a happy state of affairs. Harley-Davidson's reputation had undergone an astonishing turnaround in a few short years. What in the early eighties had been shunned as unreliable and vibratory had been transformed into desirable fashion statements, commanding a premium price. In fact, in the latter part of the decade it seemed that Harley could do no wrong. It made a $17.7 million profit in 1987, and $27

No other manufacturer could get away with this. Harley-Davidson did, and made a success of it to boot!

million the following year. A lapse into statistics may be forgiven if a few figures are quoted, comparing the beginning of the eighties to the end: productivity up by half, U.S. market share doubled; inventory cut by 75 per cent, scrap/rework down by two-thirds; a profit of $59 million. Harley-Davidson regained its traditional lead in the U.S. big bike market, grabbing almost half the share in 1988. That was twice what it had at the 1983 low point, and it is interesting to note that the recovery was almost entirely at Honda's expense. Despite the success of the Goldwing (now built in the States, funnily enough) those riders who had deserted Harley in the bad old days were now coming back.

There were other good signs. Police contracts started up again, as well. The 1985 FXRP police model took full advantage of the rubber-mounted Evolution set-up, and police riders, often disillusioned with Harleys as working bikes, had to admit that real improvements were filtering through at last, and when the California Highway Patrol chose the FXRP, it did Harley-Davidson sales in the sunshine state no harm at all. Not everyone agreed (the Los Angeles Police Dept. stayed with

Specifications

1980 FLT Tour Glide
Engine

Type	Air-cooled, 4-stroke V-twin
Capacity	82ci (1338cc)
Bore x stroke	89 x 108mm
Transmission	
Clutch	Wet, multiplate
Gearbox	5-speed
Final drive	Fully enclosed chain
Chassis	
Frame	Tubular steel, rubber mounts
Front suspension	Telescopic fork
Rear suspension	Swinging arm, twin dampers
Front brake	Twin discs, 10in (25cm).
Rear brake	Single disc, 12in (30cm).
Fuel capacity	5.0 gallons (U.S.)
Weight	725lb (329kg)

Kawasakis) and the days had certainly gone when Harley could count on a monopoly of police business; but perhaps that was no bad thing. Exports were booming too, and ever since they have formed a major part of Harley's business. Export earnings increased 177 per cent in the eighties (admittedly from a low base) and it must have caused some satisfaction when Japan became Harley-Davidson's best overseas customer.

In fact, so confident was Harley that it voluntarily requested the ITC to remove the tariff on imported bikes. In reality, the tariff had by then only a year to run, and had been reduced to 15 per cent, but it was a superb piece of publicity. Perhaps it was inevitable that this all-American success story should have had

presidential support soon afterwards. Politicians, as do most people, like to be associated with success, and Harley-Davidson was increasingly perceived to be the very model of an American company which had proved it could meet and beat global competition. Mr. Reagan toured the plant, gave a speech and started up a Sportster. ('This thing won't run away with me, will it?', he is alleged to have said.) He also remarked that Harley-Davidson was 'once again a leader in developing new motorcycle technology.' Not everyone would agree with that statement, but the important thing was not what Reagan said but that he was there at all. Harley-Davidson had become the American success story of the eighties.

Specifications

1988 Sportster 1200
Engine

Type	Air-cooled 4-stroke V-twin
Capacity	73ci (1199cc)
Bore x stroke	89 x 97mm
Compression ratio	9.0:1
Carburation	Keihin CV 40mm
Power	68bhp @ 6,000rpm
Torque	72lb ft @ 4,000rpm

Transmission

Primary drive	Duplex chain
Clutch	Multiplate, wet
Gearbox	Four-speed
Final drive	Chain

Chassis

Frame	Tubular steel
Front suspension	Telescopic fork, 39mm
Rear suspension shocks	Swinging arm, twin
Front brake disc	Single 11.5in (29cm)
Rear brake	Single 11.5in disc
Front tyre	MT90H19
Rear tyre	MT90S16
Wheelbase	60in (152cm)
Seat height	30.3in (77cm)
Fuel capacity	2.1 gallons (U.S.)
Dry weight	470lb (213kg)

Specifications

Springer Softail FXSTS (1988)
Engine

Type	Air-cooled 4-stroke V-twin
Capacity	82ci (1340cc)
Bore x stroke	88 x 108mm
Compression ratio	8.5:1
Carburetion	Keihin CV 38mm
Power	70bhp @ 5,000rpm
Torque	80lb ft 4,000rpm

Transmission

Primary drive	Duplex chain
Clutch	Multi-plate, wet
Gearbox	Five-speed
Final drive	Belt

Chassis

Frame	Tubular steel
Front suspension	Leading link type, non-adj.
Rear suspension	Twin Showa shocks, adj.
Front brake	Single 11.5in (29cm) disc
Rear brake	Single 11.5in disc
Front tyre	MH90-21
Rear tyre	MT90-16
Wheelbase	65in (165cm)
Seat height	26.5in (67cm)
Fuel capacity	4.6 gallons (US)
Dry weight	614lb (279kg)

Chapter Ten
The 1990s:
Doing Well by Looking Old

**The 1560cc Harley – Fat Boy – The FXRT – The Buell – Dyna Glide – Patent battles –
The Road King – Fuel injection – Dead end or new start?**

Most people now bought Harleys because they looked like Harleys, not just because they were good at getting from A to B.

It was a measure of Harley-Davidson's recovery that in 1990 it could call a motorcycle 'Fat Boy' and be taken seriously. Or at least, taken seriously by those who loved Harleys. And there were quite a few around who did. As the buoyant late eighties merged into the less certain nineties, the Harley bandwagon showed no sign of slowing down, and it was not just Harley fanatics who were buying the bikes. There was a new breed of affluent bikers, attracted by the powerful image, and by the Evolution's now well-proven reliability. Motorcycling was fast becoming a leisure activity, and Harley-Davidson was beginning to reap the benefits. To riders who only rode at weekends, often for short distances, it didn't matter that the Harley was slower, cruder and more expensive than any of the Japanese look-alikes. What was more important to them was that it was a big, solid all-American motorcycle.

The way that Harleys have developed in the nineties has reflected this market. Top management at York and Milwaukee has not invested a great deal in fresh engineering because it doesn't see the need. It has the resources, in plenty, to develop an all-new family of liquid-cooled engines, but instead, money has been spent on diversifying the range with new mix 'n' matches of existing components. What Willie G. did in the seventies because the company could not afford to do otherwise has become the norm simply because, for the moment at least, it still makes commercial sense.

Still, there were rumours of a 92ci (1500cc)

Evo in 1989/90 to counteract the 1400cc Japanese V-twins. Maybe journalists were reading more into events than was justified; but when bigger starter motors were fitted in 1989, and a new clutch the year after, one at least hailed this as preparing the ground for a 95ci (1560cc) twin. But it was reported in mid-1990 that the biggest twin ever had been shelved. It was said to have reached the running prototype stage, and used a longer stroke to gain the extra cubes. Apparently, it increased piston and bore wear unacceptably, and seven years later there is still no sign of the 1.5-litre Harley.

A more accurate pointer to what could be expected in the nineties was the Fat Boy. The nearest thing to a new Harley model in 1990, it was really no more than a Heritage Softail with a few styling tweaks and a new paint job. It was silver. The whole thing was silver – frame, tank, mudguards – with just a couple of yellow highlights on the engine. And since the bike was supposed to look big, solid and – well, fat – the stylists filled every gap they could find. Both wheels were solid aluminium discs, while the mudguards were wide and heavily valanced, encompassing fat 16-inch (406-mm) tyres. The handlebars were a massive 34inches (86cm) wide and there were two level 'shot gun' pipes on the right-hand side. All this was finished off with tassels on the saddle and an engraved leather strap on the tank.

The important thing about the Fat Boy (and the reason why it was the real pointer to Harley-Davidson's progress for the rest of the decade) was that it still had its big V-twin bolted directly to the frame, despite the fact that the excellent rubber mounts had been around for ten years. So vibration got through to the rider, especially if

you pushed Fat Boy beyond a gentle 60mph (97km/h) cruise. Meanwhile, lack of ground clearance and soft suspension meant that anything more than gentle cornering grounded out the floor boards. Despite all this, the Fat Boy was a great success, and it is still part of the Harley line-up in 1997.

In contrast, there is the FXRT. If the Fat Boy was Harley's nearest thing to a new model in 1990, then the FXRT was its nearest to a modern bike. It used the rubber-mounted engine; it had a decent modern fairing, air adjustable forks and twin front-disc brakes; it was lighter and easier to manage than the big FLs. The very similar FXRP had allowed Harley-Davidson to reclaim some police sales and yet Harley-Davidson sold a mere 600 civilian FXRTs in

1990, and the bike was dropped altogether three years later. The reason was simple: by now, most people bought Harleys because they looked like Harleys, not because they were good at getting from A to B, and prominent among these were celebrities of all kinds. Of course, the rich and famous had always been happy to be snapped in the saddle of a Harley-Davidson – Clark Gable was a fan – but 'Harleywood' was new – a phenomenon of the eighties and nineties. Sylvester Stallone, Bruce Springstein, Cher, Bruce Willis – the list seemed endless. Millionaire Malcolm Forbes even formed his own motorcycle club (Capitalist Tools M/C) for similarly wealthy riders. One less famous Harley rider, however, wryly observed that in Hollywood, Harley-Davidsons had come to resemble a certain part of the human anatomy – everyone had one!

In other words, there was a danger of Harleys disappearing up an over-styled back alley; but fortunately, there was Buell. Since Erik Buell and his XR1000-powered show bike had first caught Milwaukee's attention in the late eighties, things had progressed. A Sportster-powered RR1200 road bike soon followed, and the Buell went into series production, hand-built and expensive. While Harley-Davidson built around 65,000 bikes a year, Buell made 200, and the new for 1992 RS1200 cost more than any Harley and was twice the price of a Sportster 1200. What it did have (and what every Buell has had since) was Erik's own patented Uniplanar rubber mounting system. The engine hung from the lattice-work steel frame via three rubber mounts, while its vertical movement was constrained by four adjustable rods. It would, the theory went, make frame and engine a rigid whole while keeping the rear wheel in line and isolating the rider from vibration. Another uniquely Buell feature was the large monoshock, mounted horizontally under the engine, working in the opposite way to a conventional spring (i.e. when ridden over a bump, the spring extended rather than compressed). It actually worked quite well, but was rather exposed for a north European winter. By contrast, the Evolution V-twin was completely standard, allowing Buell to sell bikes without putting them through costly EPA certification.

Apart from some early reservations concerning that rear monoshock, it all seemed to work. Road tests praised the lack of vibration and the performance. (The 1200 wasn't powerful, but the Buell was lighter than the average Harley.) It had modern four-piston caliper brakes (standard Harley-Davidson brakes were becoming more of an embarrassment by the year) and up-to-the-minute WP upside-down front forks soon joined the specification list as well.

Despite the price, Buells sold well. So well, that Harley-Davidson did the obvious and bought the company, or at least 49 per cent of it. Erik Buell still had a controlling interest, but this ex-Harley-Davidson employee had to all intents and purposes rejoined the old firm. And there were plenty of advantages; engine supplies were guaranteed, and Buell now had the resources to increase production and diversify. As the nineties progressed it became clear that a Harley-powered sportsbike, however good the components used, would never be as near to the forefront of the cutting edge as the latest hyperbikes from Japan and Italy – the Honda FireBlade and Ducati 916 – which had virtually rewritten the rules of sport-bike design. Instead, Buells were transformed from the purely sporting, race-derived RS into something resembling a streetfighter custom – that is, an all-engine machine with no fairing, more for short blasts than anything else. There was also an attempt to take on the sports tourers by adding a small fairing and panniers to the basic bike. The Buell Thunderbolt certainly looked like a proper sports tourer, but road tests revealed that it really wasn't refined enough to take the mainstream bikes head-on. On the other hand, Buells had opened up the market to Harley-Davidson (at least indirectly) which appeared to have been closed to them for ever. And thanks to a move away from hand-building to something nearer mass-production, Buells were not that expensive any more; in 1997, the basic M2 Cyclone cost about the same as the top-of-the-range Sportster. Sales reflected that, from a couple of hundred bikes in 1991 to over 1,900 in 1996 and double that the year after. Harley-Davidson's investment in Buell had paid handsome dividends.

Meanwhile, the mainstream Harleys were making slow progress. In 1993, the 883 Sportsters finally acquired belt-drive and five-speed gearboxes, both of them long overdue, though this also highlighted the fact that the 883 was still a loss-leader, priced low to attract first-time Harley-Davidson buyers away from the

A Fat Boy of 1996, by which time it had lost the distinctive all-silver colour scheme but retained the solid aluminium wheels and staggered pipes. So successful is it, that it looks like lasting right through the nineties.

Harley-style Japanese cruisers. There were various Anniversary specials (it was after all 90 years since that first 1903 prototype) and the Softail theme reached its logical conclusion with the Heritage Softail 'Nostalgia' – Fat Boy 'shotgun' exhausts and wide handlebars, small leather panniers, whitewall tyres and a black-and-white colour scheme which even extended to black-and-white leather inserts for the seat. It could be regarded either as a splendid tribute to times past or a dreadful example of kitsch on two wheels, depending on one's point of view.

The new Dyna Glide was more relevant to Harley-Davidson's range for the rest of the decade. It was basically an update of the mid-range rubber-mounted FX series. Actually, 'update' is the wrong word, as the real purpose of the FXD Dyna Glide was to take Harley's most modern range and make it look as though it came from an earlier period. Just as the Softails sought to emulate the pre-rear suspension Hydra Glide of the fifties, so the Dyna paid similar homage to the original seventies Low Rider. A new single backbone frame retained the rubber mounts which so effectively isolated the engine, but used large forgings at the frame joints to create the impression of a rigid-mounted engine.

Meanwhile, to complete the look, the battery was suspended below the seat-post tube. The Dynas were to replace the FXRs from which they derived and simply underlined the fact that Harleys now had to look old-fashioned in order to sell. Even the names were full of nostalgia: the first Dyna Glide was a limited-edition 'Sturgis' and was soon followed by the raked fork, 21-inch (53-cm) front-wheeled Wide Glide. Both these names had first appeared in 1980. While environmentalists the world over were urging us to recycle, Harley was already doing it!

Mechanically, there was nothing new about the Dyna Glide. The 82ci (1340cc) Evolution twin, now into its tenth year, soldiered on with only necessary changes to accommodate legislation. As ever, it was in a low compression (8.5:1) mild state of tune, which meant just under 70bhp and with 80lb ft of torque. It would pull happily from 1,000rpm, waffle comfortably along at 60–70mph (97–113km/h) but was reluctant to cruise above 85; according to one road tester, the Dyna Glide could actually be goaded on to an indicated 110mph (177km/h), but it took a while to get there. The same rider described it as 'uncannily smooth' but ended by criticizing the Dyna as, 'too bland' for the same reason. For some, it seemed, even rubber mounting disguised as a vibey rigid frame wasn't good enough.

Harley-Davidson's heritage – the names it gave to its bikes and the way they sounded – was becoming more important than the way the bikes actually performed, and this was underlined by another development in the nineties which had very little to do with making motorcycles. With the Japanese producing large, reliable, good-looking V-twins, Harley-Davidson became increasingly jealous of the features it had that were still unique. It couldn't patent the V-twin, but certain names were registered as trade-marks – 'Glide', 'Sportster' – even 'Hog', all became Harley-Davidson property after due legal process, and woe betide anyone outside the company who used these without prior permission. Non-franchise dealers (always a bone of contention with Milwaukee) were hit hard, and one English magazine was forced (under threat of costly legal action) to change its name from Hog to Vee. Harley-Davidson even tried to adopt the defunct Indian name; one could understand the appeal of a modern Heritage with Indian Chief badges, and with the Indian name in legal limbo there was always the possibility of a highly plausible Honda Chief. This was prevented, however, by an outcry from the ranks of Indian bike owners.

But perhaps the most extraordinary part of Harley's patent frenzy was the 'potato-potato' saga. More than once it attempted to patent the sound made by its motorcycles. This was actually based, not on a subjective description of cadence and rolling thunder, but engineering principles. It was undeniable that the distinctive off-beat sound of a Harley (particularly at idle) was down to its 45-degree cylinder angle, with the two connecting rods sharing a common crankpin. The actual layout was an historical accident – Harley had simply stuck with this arrangement, while all the more recent V-twin rivals have gone for a more functional wider angle and side-by-side con-rods. The application stated: 'The Harley-Davidson sound functions as a [trade] mark and identifies Harley-Davidson alone as the source of the goods emitting that sound.' Whatever you think of what must be a world-first in patent history, one thing was clear – the importance to Harley-Davidson of its image, rather than how fast or comfortable or advanced its bikes were.

Just as the Dyna Glide harked back to the FX-series, so did the 1994 Road King to the basic FL Electra Glide. The FLs had long been losing out in sales to the more obviously retrospective Heritage Softails. So the new-fangled bar-mounted speedometer was moved back to its traditional position on top of the tank. It was joined there by switchgear, with the whole lot mounted in a large chrome console; it could almost have been a Knucklehead – but that was the idea. The handlebar fairing went, replaced by a quick-release screen and massive chrome headlamp nacelle. The pillion portion of the seat was also quickly detachable (via one screw) to

A contrast in styles: the Softail Custom (left) displays its raked forks and higher bars next to a Heritage Softail on Daytona Beach. Under the skin, however, both are very similar.

improvement, unless you were of the more reactionary 'keep it simple' brigade. The electronic system was up-to-the-minute, with a central ECU which fuelled the engine according to temperature, load and so on – there was even a diagnostic function. Cars had used systems like this for years, but they were only just starting to appear on expensive motorcycles; Harley-Davidson's engineering department was taking note of goings-on in the outside world, after all.

The Sportster 1200 was split into two for 1996, the XL1200 Sport bringing a more sporting chassis to the standard Evo power train. There were twin discs, fully adjustable suspension (piggyback gas reservoirs on the back), alloy wheels and flatter bars. A couple of years on and it even got some extra power as well, with twin-plug heads, higher compression and new cams. It was a sign of the times though that the 1998 catalogue quoted only torque figures; Harley-Davidson's power figures had fallen too far

Specifications

1990 Fat Boy
Engine

Type	Air-cooled 4-stroke V-twin
Capacity	82ci (1340cc)
Bore x stroke	89 x 108mm
Compression ratio	8.5:1
Power	72bhp @ 5,200rpm
Torque	83lb ft @ 4,000rpm
Transmission	
Gearbox	5-speed
Final drive	Toothed belt
Chassis	
Frame	Tubular steel
Front suspension	41mm telescopic fork
Rear suspension	Swinging arm, twin hidden dampers
Front brake	Single disc
Rear brake	Single disc
Front tyre	MT90 S16
Wheelbase	62.5in (159cm)
Seat height	26in (66cm)
Fuel capacity	4.5 gallons (U.S.)
Fuel consumption	40mpg (14km per litre) average

The Springer Softail sums up Harley-Davidson's strategy for the nineties pretty well. Despite adequate resources to develop all-new, thoroughly modern bikes, it chooses to trade on the past. And why not? It has made profits, created employment, and kept a lot of riders happy.

give an authentically fifties large solo saddle.

There were even some mechanical improvements, though these were shared by all the 1995 model year Glides. Power and torque got a slight but much needed boost from a remapped ignition system, better breathing and larger silencers. On the road, the changes seemed to have made a difference, and these latest big twins were both faster and used less fuel than those of the previous year. In fact, it seemed as if Harley-Davidson was at last realizing that the Evo itself needed some serious evolution. A year later, fuel injection appeared. Fitted at first only on the U.S./Canadian market Electra Glide Ultra (which now became the FLHTCI) it increased maximum torque to 83lb ft (from 77lb ft) as well as improving economy and cold starting. Oddly, by 1998, Harley-Davidson was claiming a mere 70lb ft of torque for the injection Evo, while the carburettored version had 75lb ft. The injection wasn't a performance aid but it was a definite behind to be spelled out in black and white, even if it didn't matter that much any more.

Meanwhile, the XL1200 Custom used the milder chassis (single disc, non-adjustable suspension) with extra chrome and higher bars. Among the big bikes, fuel injection spread to the standard Electra Glide, and it can only be a matter of time now before it trickles down to all the big twins. The Sportsters, being more price sensitive (especially the 883s) are less likely to use injection unless legislation demands it.

There were failures as well: an all-black Springer named 'Bad Boy' didn't last long but, in general, the Harley-Davidson bandwagon rolls on. Recently there have been accusations that the company is heading up a blind alley, taking its mix 'n' match marketing too far at the expense of engineering. However, there are two reasons for optimism. One, it seems determined to keep the 883 Sportster as an entry-level bike, rather than be tempted by big profit margins on expensive

machines. The current U.K. specification Sportster costs just under £5,000, undercutting some of the Japanese competition, and that is essential if new riders are to continue to be attracted to the Harley fold. The second reason is the VR1000 racer which made its debut at Daytona in 1994. Harley-Davidson would rather forget that first outing when the VR qualified eight seconds behind the Ducatis, and lasted less than half the distance, and the next two years showed it to be far from the race-winner many hoped it would be. But the important thing about the VR was its specification. Admittedly designed by a team outside the factory, this liquid-cooled 60-degree V-twin had fuel injection, overhead cams and four valves per cylinder. Could it be that there will be a mildly tuned, touring development of this engine powering a new generation of Harleys for the new Millenium? Or perhaps Harley-Davidson's 100th Anniversary will be the Evolution's 20th year in production. What do you think?

Specifications

1998 Electra Glide Ultra Classic
Engine

Type	Air-cooled, 4-stroke V-twin
Capacity	82ci (1338cc)
Bore x stroke	89 x 108mm
Fuelling	Electronic injection
Power	Not quoted
Torque	70lb ft @ 3,000rpm

Transmission

Clutch	Wet, multiplate
Gearbox	Five-speed
Final drive	Toothed belt

Chassis

Frame	Tubular steel
Front suspension	Telescopic fork
Rear suspension	Swinging arm, twin dampers
Front brake	Twin discs
Rear brake	Single disc
Front tyre	MT90-16
Rear tyre	MT90-16
Seat height	27.7in (70cm)
Fuel capacity	4.2 gallons (U.S.)
Weight	748lb (339kg)

Specifications

1998 Sportster 1200S
Engine

Type	Air-cooled 4-stroke V-twin
Capacity	73ci (1199cc)
Bore x stroke	89 x 97mm
Fuelling	Single carburettor
Power	Not quoted
Torque	66lb ft @ 3,500rpm

Transmission

Clutch	Wet, multiplate
Gearbox	Five-speed
Final drive	Toothed belt

Chassis

Frame	Tubular steel
Front suspension	Telescopic fork, adj.
Rear suspension	Swinging arm, twin dampers, adj.
Front brake	Twin discs
Rear brake	Single disc
Front tyre	100/90-19
Rear tyre	130/90-16
Seat height	29.3in (74cm)
Fuel capacity	2.8 gallons (U.S.)
Weight	517lb (235kg)